GOOD HOUSEKEEPING
QUICK HOME REPAIRS

GOOD HOUSEKEEPING
QUICK
HOME
REPAIRS

Good Housekeeping Institute

EBURY PRESS
LONDON

Published by Ebury Press
National Magazine House
72 Broadwick Street
London W1V 2BP

First impression 1982

ISBN 0 85223 220 9 (hardback)
ISBN 0 85223 216 0 (paperback)

Text: Cassandra Kent
Research: Gill Smedley, Jack Smith
Illustrations: John Woodcock

Filmset by Advanced Filmsetters (Glasgow) Limited
Printed in Great Britain at the
University Press, Cambridge

CONTENTS

FOREWORD

There's nothing more frustrating than small repair jobs around the home that you're sure you could put right quickly and simply if only you knew how. Most home repairs are within the scope of the householder, even without previous DIY experience, and this book will not only tell you how to put things right, but also what products to use to ensure perfect results. All the repairs in this book have been carried out by members of the Good Housekeeping Institute staff, and all the products mentioned have been thoroughly tested.

Before you start, read through the instructions for each repair carefully, taking particular note of any safety rules, and ensuring you have the necessary tools and equipment. If any of the techniques referred to are unfamiliar, consult a detailed do-it-yourself or decorating manual for full instructions.

The Good Housekeeping Institute is happy to deal with any queries arising from this book provided they are accompanied by a stamped, addressed envelope. Letters sent without an *sae* will not receive a reply. Write to:

GOOD HOUSEKEEPING INSTITUTE
National Magazine House
72 Broadwick Street
London W1V 2BP

WALLS AND CEILINGS

Covering stained patches caused by damp

First check the source of the trouble and attend to it.

Stains on walls or ceilings should be painted with a coat of oil-based undercoat or aluminium primer (from department stores and DIY shops) before redecorating.

Badly stained surfaces may also need covering with lining paper before redecorating.

Covering rough surfaces

If a surface has hairline cracks and small pits, the easiest solution is to paper it. If you want to cover a rough area without filling or using a lining paper, apply **Polyripple** by **Polycell**. This is a surface covering that gives a rippled effect and covers over most minor imperfections. It comes in 2.5- and 5-litre tubs from DIY shops and Woolworth's and can be emulsion painted the colour of your choice.

Plugging drill holes that are too large

When drilling into old or crumbly walls, it is often impossible to prevent the holes from becoming ragged and larger than intended. Use an all-purpose filler such as **Tetrion** to fill the hole before inserting a plug and/or screw.

Dealing with badly papered walls

The perfectionist's solution to this problem is to strip off the old paper and start from scratch. Failing this, if you are going to emulsion over paper that curves round internal corners, carefully slit it down the centre and stick the edges down, overlapping if necessary. Fill any rough areas with **Interior Polyfilla**, smoothed off with fine glasspaper to leave a good surface to paint over. You usually need at least two coats of paint.

8

Filling hairline cracks in plaster

First enlarge the crack with the edge of a filler knife in order to provide a firm grip for the filler. Remove dust from the opening with a soft brush (or use the crevice tool of a vacuum cleaner).

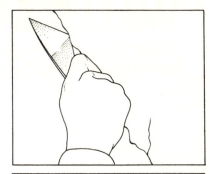

Apply a filler, such as **Interior Polyfilla**, pushing it into the crack firmly with a filler knife or small trowel and leaving it slightly proud of the surrounding wall to allow for shrinkage as it dries. Deep cracks may need two applications of filler.

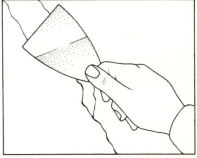

When dry, rub the filler down with fine glasspaper on a small block until it is level with the rest of the wall.

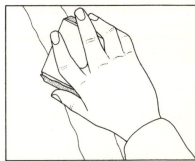

Filling large holes in plaster

It is uneconomical to fill large holes in the same way as small holes or cracks, ie with cellulose filler. Large holes require you to build up the cavity first. Soak crumpled newspaper in water, then dip it in a plaster solution made up to the consistency of double cream. Use the newspaper to fill the hole in the wall, then use a hand trowel to cover this 'plug' with a layer of plaster. Leave to dry, then apply a second coat, leaving it slightly proud of the surrounding surface. Allow the plaster to dry thoroughly before smoothing off with fine glasspaper.

Patching chipped plaster on protruding corners

Corners of some alcoves or chimney breasts and other protruding areas are often easily damaged when moving furniture or decorating.

For large areas of damage you will need to fix a metal edging or corner bead (from DIY shops). Trim away the damaged plaster and smooth off with glasspaper so that the bead lies flush with the rest of the wall. Fix it into position with small dabs of plaster.

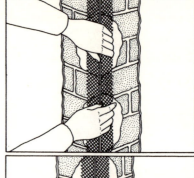

Use a spirit level to check that it is vertical and use a batten or ruler to check that it is flush with the surrounding wall surfaces.

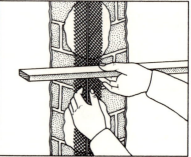

When it is fixed, apply a thin layer of plaster to cover it and leave to dry out thoroughly. Rub down with glass-paper to smooth over the area before decorating.

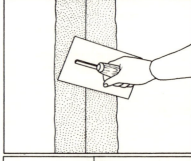

Smaller areas of damage can be repaired by applying a filler, such as **Interior Polyfilla**, in thin layers until it is slightly proud of the damage. Nail a batten flush to the corner with some masonry nails, taking care not to cause further damage in doing so. This will provide a firm edge against which to build up the layers of filler. Leave one side of the corner to dry before working on the other side.

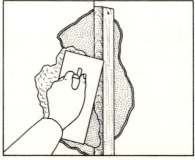

When both sides are dry, rub the filler down to shape with glasspaper. Do not use an electric sanding attachment as this can damage good surrounding plaster. Any holes left by the masonry nails can also be filled with **Polyfilla** and sanded down when dry.

Eliminating the smell from newly hung vinyl wallcoverings

There is nothing you can do to avoid this problem in the first place, but it helps if the room is as well ventilated as possible while the vinyl is being hung and for some time afterwards. Once the adhesive is thoroughly dry the smell will disappear in time.

Refixing vinyl wallcoverings

Vinyl wallcoverings that have become unstuck at the seams can be glued down again with **Solvite Overlap and Repair Adhesive** which will stick vinyl to walls or vinyl to vinyl where the wallcovering has been overlapped. If large sections of the wallcovering have become unstuck, it will be necessary to take it down and replace it with new.

Patching wallcoverings

Wallpaper Tear away the damaged area leaving an unevenly shaped hole with a layered edge of paper all round. This is easier to disguise than an evenly cut edge. From a spare roll of matching paper, tear a patch which will fit over the area and match the surrounding paper. The patch should be larger than the damaged area.

Apply wallpaper paste to the patch and carefully ease it into position. To ensure that the edges are well stuck, press them with a clean dry cloth or wallpaper seam roller.

Vinyl or Fabric Wallcoverings Vinyl or fabric wallcoverings cannot be torn so you should cut a matching piece larger than the damaged area. Place it over the damaged area and, with a sharp knife, cut through both the patch and the wallcovering so that a neat hole and a neat patch are produced. Peel off the damaged wallcovering and, in the case of vinyl wallpaper, the lining paper which will probably not come away from the wall when you first peel it off, and stick in the new patch with an appropriate adhesive.

Sticking self-adhesive hooks on effectively

Most self-adhesive hooks fall off because they are stuck on to poor surfaces. You cannot fix a self-adhesive hook on to a porous surface, such as brick or bare plaster, or one with flaking paintwork.

It is essential that the surface is both clean and dry before you apply the hook. If it is to be fixed to a ceramic tile, first clean the tile with white spirit, wipe it with a damp cloth and dry it thoroughly.

Reducing noise from next door

If noise from your neighbours is a problem there is really not much a handyman can do about it. Noise prevention measures tend to be expensive, need professional installation and are not always very effective.

Write for the free booklet *Sound Insulation in your Home* from British Gypsum Ltd, Westfield, 360 Singlewell Road, Gravesend, Kent DA11 7RZ, which may provide suggestions to solve your particular problem.

Repairing a cracked fireback

Do not attempt to repair a fireback for at least 48 hours after having had a fire in the grate. Close the damper, if there is one, and brush or vacuum up dirt and ashes. Soak the damaged area with water. Score the crack with a trowel to enlarge it and provide a good grip for the cement and fill it with a fire cement such as **Templer's** or **Purimachos** (from builders' merchants or DIY shops) while it is still damp. Smooth off the excess filler with the trowel, wet your finger and rub the cement gently until you achieve the right finish. Leave the cement to set for at least 24 hours before lighting a fire.

Sweeping a chimney

While it is possible to do this yourself with hired tools it is only slightly more expensive and a lot more satisfactory to employ a professional sweep. Look in your Yellow Pages directory or contact your local Solid Fuel Advisory Service (under S in the telephone directory) for a list of sweeps in your area.

Book a sweep well in advance to give you time to prepare the room. Remove ornaments and loose rugs and cover the furniture with dust sheets. Be prepared to have to clean the whole room thoroughly after the chimney has been swept.

Remember . . .

Always remove old wallcovering before putting up new.

Never perch on a stool or chair to reach a high place—use a stable step ladder or a trestle.

Never use dirty paintbrushes or you will spoil the finish of your paintwork. Clean them out after each use and store them in a clean dry place.

Use wet or dry abrasive paper when rubbing down old paintwork. If moistened in water, it will prevent dust flying about.

Never try to decorate *around* furniture! Clear the room as far as possible and protect any furniture that can't be moved by covering it with a dust sheet.

Although time-consuming, preparation is 90% of the job. Do it properly and you will obtain a satisfactory result. Failure to prepare correctly will produce a less than perfect finish.

After preparing them, ensure that all surfaces are clean and dry before starting work.

Before applying emulsion paint over wallpaper, do a test on a small inconspicuous area to check the paint will adhere and give the colour you want. Bear in mind that painting over wallpaper makes it more difficult to remove when stripping becomes necessary.

Carry out major repairs, such as repairing window frames or removing a fireplace, before starting on the basic preparation work for decorating.

WINDOWS AND DOORS

Filling cracks and chips in woodwork

Use either **Interior Polyfilla** or ready-mixed **Fine Surface Polyfilla** applied with a flexible scraper. When it is dry, rub the new surface down lightly with fine glasspaper until flush with the surrounding paint. Prime and paint.

Treating knots in wood

Knots in new wood are usually surrounded by a resinous substance which is dissolved by the solvents in paint and will eventually appear as brown marks on the surface of the paint. You can prevent this by coating the surface of each knot before priming and painting. Use a proprietary knotting compound (from hardware and DIY shops).

Draughtproofing doors and casement windows

The easiest way to do this is to fit a foam tape such as **Marley Multi-purpose Foam Tape**, which has a self-adhesive backing, around the door or window frames. It is most effective in small gaps on wooden or metal frames but not for sliding windows or doors. It has a life of only one or two seasons. A tougher type which is guaranteed for five years is **Scandy Super Weatherstrip**.

When filling larger gaps, use a tubular strip set in a rigid plastic or metal section, such as **OBO Doorset Draught Excluder**. This has to be fixed to the frame with panel pins.

Removing paint from window glass

Small scrapers fitted with razor blades are available from DIY shops specifically for this purpose. When using, hold the blade almost flat against the glass in order to avoid scratching it. Clean the windows by your usual method.

Removing rust from metal windows

Use a chemical rust remover such as **Kurust**. Wear goggles and gloves and take care not to get any on your skin. Brush or wash off any loose rust, grease and dust from the surface and leave it to dry. Apply the remover with an old paintbrush and leave it to work for 10–15 minutes.

Clean it off according to the manufacturer's instructions. Allow the surface to dry thoroughly and paint. It is not usually necessary to use a primer when a chemical rust remover has been applied.

Securing loose glass in a window frame

Glass can become loose when putty on the outside of the window deteriorates and falls out. If possible, remove the window from its frame or take it off its hinges as this will make the job easier.

Rake out the loose putty using a sharp wood chisel. Carefully clean the rebate, ensuring that you do not break the glass. Brush on a thin layer of undercoat or wood primer, allow to dry and apply new putty. Smooth off the putty with a putty knife and leave a steep angle so that rain and moisture will run off. Leave the putty to dry for a week before painting.

Dealing with rotting window frames

With wooden window frames it is sometimes possible to replace a small damaged section but this is usually a job for a professional builder or carpenter.

In general, wooden and metal frames need to be replaced once they begin to deteriorate. New ones may be wood, aluminium or uPVC (rigid plastic). Aluminium or uPVC frames do not need painting. Make sure you deal with a reputable firm that is a member of the Glass and Glazing Federation. Write to them for a list of members in your area (see page 118) or to the British Woodworking Federation (see page 117), enclosing a stamped addressed envelope for their reply.

Curing a rattle in a casement window

This normally occurs because the catch plate on the window frame has worn. If it is the spindle that holds the handle of the casement fastener that has worn, you will need to replace the whole fastener. You should be able to match the existing ones at **Knobs & Knockers** (in Debenham stores or see page 119). A mail order catalogue is available. Send a stamped addressed envelope.

Alternatively, all you may need to do is unscrew the catch plate and move it in to take up the slack. You may have to chisel out a slight recess in the frame for the front of the catch to enter. Fill the old screw holes in the frame with tapering softwood plugs glued into place with a wood-working adhesive such as **Evo-Stik**. Sand flush and paint to match the rest of the frame.

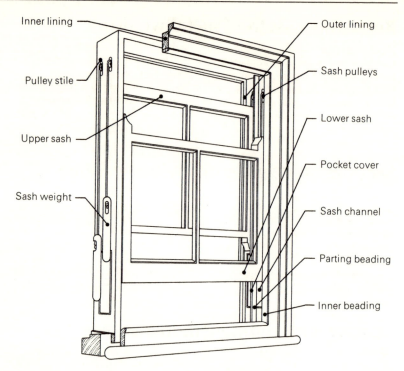

Inner lining

Pulley stile

Upper sash

Sash weight

Outer lining

Sash pulleys

Lower sash

Pocket cover

Sash channel

Parting beading

Inner beading

Curing a rattle in a sash window

A fairly major repair is usually needed but, as a temporary measure, you can wedge the sashes in their frame with plastic wedges (available in packs of two from Woolworth's and hardware shops) or wads of cardboard.

For a permanent job you will need to renew the parting beading that forms the sash channels (see above). Prise off the inner beading from all round the window, remove the lower sash and pull the parting beads out of their grooves. Measure up for new beading. Insert the new lengths of parting bead, replace the lower sash and refix the original inner beads in position. Check that the sashes run smoothly and paint the new beading.

If this repair is needed on an upstairs window, it is advisable to have expert help.

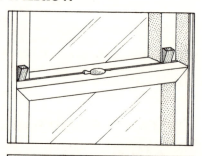

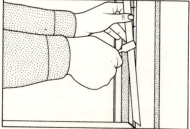

Reglazing a wooden window

Wear protective gloves and goggles and, standing on the outside of the window, carefully remove all the broken glass by tapping it out lightly with a hammer. Wrap the pieces well in old newspaper before putting them in the dustbin.

Using a chisel, clean out all the old putty from the rebate (the groove which holds the glass in place), taking care not to damage the frame.

Measure up for the new glass by measuring the length of all four sides. Old window frames are often not square. Draw a sketch showing all the dimensions, including the diagonals. Be sure to order the correct thickness of glass. Your glass supplier will be able to advise you.

Apply primer to the bare wood and then press a layer of all-purpose putty into the rebate. Place the glass in position, applying pressure only round the edges, not in the centre or it will crack. When the putty starts to squeeze out this indicates that the glass is correctly bedded in.

Gently hammer two or three glazing nails along each edge of the frame to hold the glass in position. Use a lightweight hammer.

Trim off the excess putty from the inside of the frame, leaving neatly finished edges. With a putty knife apply a layer of putty all round the outside edge of the frame so that rain will run off.

Leave the putty to dry for at least a week before painting. Apply the paint to the putty and just over the edge so that it forms a seal with the glass.

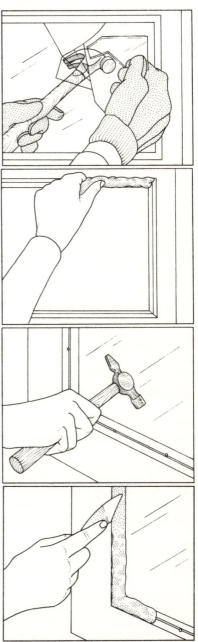

Reglazing a metal window

The glass in metal windows is held in place with putty and wire spring clips rather than the glazing pins used for wooden window frames. Remove broken glass very carefully, wearing thick gloves, scrape out the putty and retain the clips, making sure you understand how they were fitted. Clean out the clip holes and the metal rebate. Remove any rust with a wire brush and apply a coat of metal primer (from DIY or paint shops) to prevent further rust occurring.

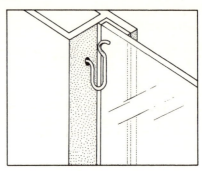

Using a metal casement putty (available from DIY shops and glass merchants), prepare a thin bed for the new glass. (Do not use ordinary oil-based putty to glaze metal windows.) Have the new piece of glass cut to the correct size, making sure that it is of the same type and thickness as the broken pane. Press the glass into position, fit the clips back firmly and then putty over the clips, smoothing off with a putty knife at an angle which will allow the rain to run off. Mitre the corners.

Replacing glass in sliding metal-framed windows should be done by professionals as the strains imposed on the glass are greater and the glass will crack if it is not fitted correctly.

Fully glazed doors and low level window panes should be fitted with safety glass (laminated or toughened glass). Enquire about this at your glass merchant.

Replacing glass in leaded lights

The panes in leaded light windows are held in place by double or single lead channels known as cames. To replace a broken pane, cut the four corners of the surrounding lead on the inside of the window with a pair of sharp scissors or metal snips (it's fairly soft) and fold back the edges. Open the window and tap out the glass from the outside of the window. If you can't get at the outside easily, carefully lever out the glass with a chisel. Clean out any loose matter from the grooves.

Make a template from a piece of cardboard. Hold it against the space and rub with a wax crayon to give the outline. Cut the shape out and test fit it in the cames. Get a glazier to cut a piece of glass fractionally smaller than the template.

Put a layer of metal casement putty (available from DIY shops and glass merchants) in the grooves and press the new glass into place. Fold the lead back over the new pane, scrape off excess putty and smooth the lead into position with the round handle of a screwdriver. Rub the outside of the lead corner joints with medium glasspaper and apply a little solder to the inside cut corners with flux and a moderately hot soldering iron. (Use a circular motion to match the other joints.) This will stop the new pane leaking when it rains.

Making a temporary window

You may need to fill the gap left by a broken pane while you arrange for its repair. Buy enough polythene sheet (from hardware shops or department stores) to cover the area with an allowance of a few centimetres all the way round. From 25 ×6-mm wood battening, cut four pieces to fit the dimensions of the window frame.

Nail the polythene sheet along the top of the window frame by fixing the top batten over it with panel pins running through both the batten and the sheeting.

Repeat with the sides and bottom edge, keeping the polythene taut.

Bear in mind that although this will keep the weather out, it can easily be slashed by an intruder, especially on a ground floor. Treat it as a temporary repair and get the window glazed as soon as possible.

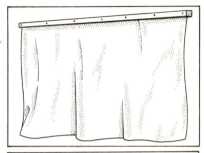

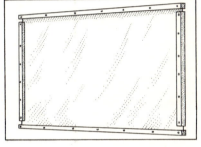

Easing a paint-stuck window

Where new paint has hardened between the side of the window and the frame, you must first prise them apart either by wedging a thin scraper between frame and sash or by tapping lightly all around the frame with a wooden mallet. Protect the paintwork with a piece of cardboard or with a duster tied round the head of the mallet.

When the layers of paint have yielded, push the window up and down or in and out and smooth off the sides and frame of the window with glasspaper.

If a casement window has warped and is sticking, you must plane or sand a small amount from the sides, bottom or top of the window where it is catching on the window frame. Oil any hinges to ensure the window opens and closes easily.

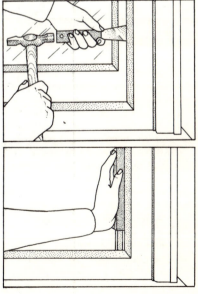

Replacing sash cords

Frayed or broken sash cords make it almost impossible to open or close a window. Replacing them is a fiddly business so it is sensible to do all four cords even if only one has actually broken.

First, remove the inner beading round the window (see page 16). Prise it off carefully using an old chisel or broad screwdriver.

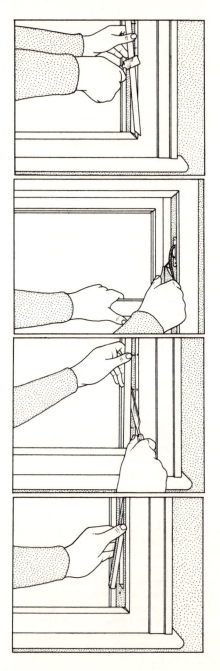

If the cords are still intact, push the bottom window up to lower the weights in the channels, and cut the cords near the pulleys at the top. Lift the lower window out.

Remove the parting strip that separates the two windows by prising it off with an old chisel, push the upper window up, cut the cords if necessary, and take the upper window out.

Remove the weight pocket covers at the bottom of the window and lift out the weights. Slip the old cords from the eyes in the weights. Cut new cords to measure, using the old ones as a guide. Check that the pulleys at the tops of the weight channels are revolving freely and, if necessary, lubricate with **Rocket WD40** (available from hardware and car accessory shops).

Pass the new cords through the pulleys and down the channels to the weight pockets at the bottom. It is easier to do this if you tie a length of string to the end of the cord and something small but heavy, such as a nail, to the end of the string. Drop the nail and string down through the channel and use the string to pull the cord through. Taking care to secure the top end of the cord so that it doesn't pass through the pulley, thread the bottom end of the cord through the eye of the weight and knot it tightly.

Nail the other end of the cord into the groove up the sides of each sash.
  Replace the weight pocket covers and fit the upper sash back into the frame. Replace the parting strip before fitting the lower sash into the frame. Finally, refix the inner beading.

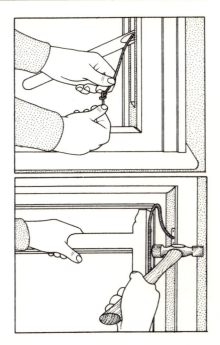

Repainting a blistered door

Doors with paint in good condition just need washing and light sanding before you apply a new coat of paint.
  Doors with blistered or defective paintwork should have the paint removed with a chemical stripper such as **Strypit Paint Remover** (follow the instructions carefully) or with a blowlamp such as the **Taymar LG870** fitted with a paint remover burner with a wide nozzle. Exercise great caution when handling a

blowlamp. Remember to keep the nozzle at least 70 mm away from the paintwork to avoid burning the wood, and keep the blowlamp moving from side to side. Do not use a blowlamp to strip paintwork close to glass. After removing the paint, wipe the door down thoroughly with a damp cloth and sand with glass-paper to give an even surface. Apply primer, undercoat and topcoat.

Rectifying hinges set too deep

When hinges are set too deep they will not keep the door shut. Unscrew the hinges on the frame side of the door and cut pieces of cereal packet card or hardboard (depending on the amount the hinges need raising) exactly the same size as the hinge recesses. Place behind the hinges as

packing and replace the hinges.
  If this is not sufficient, repeat the process on the door side of the hinge. If the screw holes have become too big, pack them with matchsticks or wall plugs glued in place with a PVA adhesive such as **Evo-Stik Woodworking Adhesive**.

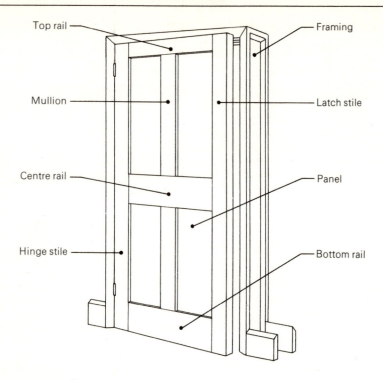

Top rail — Framing

Mullion — Latch stile

Centre rail — Panel

Hinge stile — Bottom rail

Resizing doors

Doors that are too small It is possible to build up a door to the correct size with strips of wood.

Take the door off its hinges and strip off any paint left on the edges of the door. Measure the door to check it is square, remove the lock and any other bolts or handles, and fill in the holes with plastic wood. Cut a length of softwood, or thin laths of wood, to fit the length and width of the latch edge of the door and thick enough to make the door slightly bigger than necessary so that it can gradually be planed down to the precise size. Fix the wood strip to the latch edge of the door with a wood glue, such as **Evo-Stik Woodworking Adhesive**, and then nail it lightly into position. If necessary, fix strips of wood to the top and bottom of the door as well.

When the glue is dry, punch the nail heads down with a hammer and nail punch and sand down any rough edges. Hold the door up in the frame to see if it fits, then plane down any excess until the door is the right size. Rehang the door, fill any holes or gaps with wood filler and sand down the whole door before repainting.

Doors that are too large If you have a door that is too large for the doorway you want it to fit, remove the lock, etc., and fill the holes with wood filler. Hold the door up in the frame and mark on it where it needs to be made smaller. If the door is more than 18 mm too big, saw off the surplus, but if the surplus is only slight it can be planed down. Fit hinges and rehang the door.

22

Correcting a sagging door

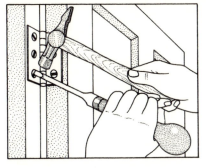 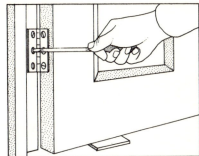

First, try tightening the screws that hold the hinges. If this doesn't solve the problem, you will need to replace the hinges.

If the screws holding the old ones have corroded, give them a tap on the head with a screwdriver and hammer. If they are still difficult to remove, drip a little **3-in-One** penetrating oil or vinegar on to the screwheads and leave for an hour or two until they soften their grip. If the screw holes have become worn and thus too large, fill them either with slivers of wood or fibre wall plugs. Glue these into the holes with a woodworking adhesive and, when dry, saw them off flush with a fine tenon saw and smooth down the ends with glasspaper.

Fix the new hinges and rehang the door.

Curing creaking hinges

Drip a couple of drops of an oil such as **3-in-One** on to the top of the hinge. Lubricate sparingly and wipe off any surplus.

Reglazing a broken door panel

Remove the old glass carefully; wear gardening gloves to protect your hands. Clear out all the putty with an old wood chisel or stiff backed knife. Remove any surrounding beading.

Measure up for the new glass and obtain it from a glazier. It is a good idea to fit safety glass (ask your glass merchant about this) if there is any risk of people walking into the door. Put a layer of putty in the rebate and smooth it out with a putty knife. Push the new glass in firmly, pressing around the edges, *not* on the centre.

When it is well bedded into the putty, tap a few glazing nails round the edge to hold it in place and finish off with a neat layer of putty. On external doors, angle the putty sharply with the putty knife so that the rain will run off.

If you do not want a putty finish on an internal door, use glazing bead (quadrant beading with a lip) fixed with panel pins. Cut the four lengths to fit and mitre the corners. Drill small holes for the pins and fix the beading into position.

23

Replacing an internal door

On the new door, saw off the sections that project at the top and bottom of the stiles (see page 22) and sand down the areas to make them smooth. Hold the door in position with the hanging edge of the door in the rebate on the hanging side of the frame.

With a soft pencil, mark where cutting or planing is necessary. Allow for a final clearance all round of 2 mm, with 3 mm at the bottom. Take the door down again and, using a sharp smoothing plane, deal in rotation with the hanging edge of the door, then the top, then the other edge. Remove a little at a time and keep a constant check by holding the door up in the frame. Finish by planing a slight slope towards the inside edges of the hanging and closing (vertical) edges of the door.

Plane the bottom of the door last. Place the door in the frame and raise it with thin wedges placed underneath until the gap at the top is slightly less than 2 mm. Plane until the final clearance at the bottom of the door is 3 mm. Allow for any additional clearance if you intend to lay floor covering afterwards.

If there are hinge position marks on the door frame, place the door in the frame and mark corresponding positions on the new door. If you are fitting new hinges, position them approximately 180 mm from the bottom and 130 mm from the top.

Take the door down, hold a hinge leaf against the edge of it and mark its outline with a pencil.
Chisel out the areas to the thickness of the hinge so that the hinge will fit flush with the door. Screw the hinges into the recesses on the door with one screw only in each.

Wedge the door in position in the frame allowing for the correct

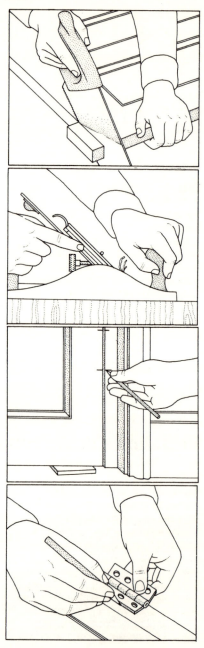

clearance all round. Check that the hinges on the door match with the position marks on the frame. If you need to make new hinge recesses in the frame leave the loose leaf of the hinge outside the frame as an aid to marking the positions.

Screw the hinges to the frame with one central screw only in each. Test the door for easy opening and closing before making final adjustments and fitting the remaining screws.

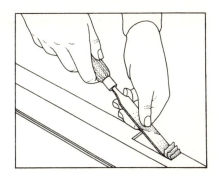

Easing a sticking door

This can have several causes:

Paint build-up This is common in older houses. Strip off all the old paint from door and frame with a chemical stripper or blowlamp (see page 21), or take the door to a professional who will strip it in a caustic bath. Wipe the woodwork with a damp cloth, smooth off with glasspaper and remove all dust. Repaint frame and door with primer, undercoat and topcoat.

New carpets A new carpet in a room where there wasn't one when the door was hung, can catch against the bottom of the door. Carefully mark the door, then remove it from its hinges and either plane off a little at the base or fit it with rising-butt hinges (see page 26) which will lift the door slightly as it opens.

Damp In a damp house, swelling can cause a door to jam in its frame or even fail to close. Mark the problem areas on the door, remove it from its hinges, plane down the parts where it is sticking and rehang it. Touch up the planed areas with matching paint. If it's an exterior door, prime the bare wood before repainting. Remember that the wood may shrink again in warm, dry weather so be careful not to plane too much off.

Note that if you have a number of doors which need their bases planing or cutting, it will be quicker and you will find it less tiring to hire a small DIY electric saw.

Worn hinges If worn or distorted hinges are the problem, swopping them from top to bottom will some-times help. If this does not solve the problem it will be necessary to fit new hinges.

Locks If it is the lock which is catching and causing the door to stick, either replace the lock spring or fit a new lock.

When easing a door using any of these remedies, it may be necessary to reposition the lock and handles, or the lock plate in the door frame, after making the adjustments.

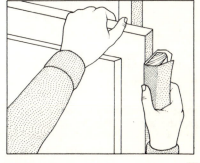

Fitting rising-butt hinges

Rising-butt hinges make it possible to open a door over a thick carpet without sawing or planing down the bottom of the door. Buy the correct type to fit the door, depending on whether it opens on the left- or right-hand side. Remove the door from its frame by unscrewing the hinges in the frame, and remove the old hinges from the door.

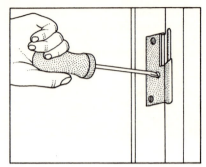

Enlarge the hinge recesses on the door with a chisel so that the new hinges will fit flush with the surface of the wood. Fit the sections of the new hinges without spindles on to the door, using one screw only for each.

Hold the door up in its frame (you may need help with this) and mark the positions for the new hinges on the frame. Using just one screw for each, screw the spindle sections of the new hinges into the frame.

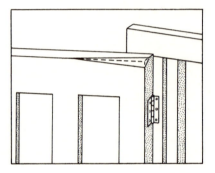

Before lifting the door on to its new hinges, use a plane to trim off a bevelled section from the top inside edge, on the hinge side, of the door. This section should be about 2.5 cm deep and 30 cm long and should slope towards the top of the door frame. This will allow the door to rise without grinding into the frame.

Hang the door on the new hinges. If it is still rubbing against the top of the frame, plane a little more wood from the top of the door. When it fits properly, put the remainder of the screws into the hinges and tighten them all up.

Easing difficult curtain runners

Remove both the curtains and the runners. Wipe over the rail with a damp cloth to remove dust and dirt and dry with a soft cloth. Apply a little wax polish to the rail and buff up, or use an aerosol lubricant such as **Rocket WD40** (available from hardware stores and car accessory shops) applied on a cloth. Wipe off any surplus, refix and rehang the curtains.

Lubricating a roller blind

If a roller blind will not stay down it probably needs lubricating. Remove it from the brackets and hold it upright with the spring mechanism (the protruding square central bar) uppermost. Protect the blind fabric with a paper towel and spray the bar with a short burst of aerosol lubricant such as **Rocket WD40**. Leave the roller in the upright position for a few minutes to allow the lubricant to run down inside. Clean the wall brackets and spray with lubricant before repositioning the blind.

Restoring the roll to a roller blind

A new roller blind may not roll up and down correctly for a variety of reasons. Check that the brackets are level and (if you have made it yourself) that the material has been cut absolutely square and that the top edge is attached squarely to the roller.

If these are all in order you need to 'tension' the blind. Take the roller blind off the brackets and wind up the spring mechanism (the square piece of metal on the left-hand end of the roller). Give it a few turns, holding on to it firmly so it does not unwind, and immediately put the blind back into the brackets. Take care not to overwind or you will weaken the spring and shorten the life of the blind.

Pull the blind down and let it up slowly a few times until the action is smooth.

Another way to tension a roller blind is to pull the blind down a short way, then lift it off the left-hand bracket and wind it up by hand. Replace the blind in the bracket and pull it down again. Repeat this until the blind works smoothly. This technique should be reversed if the blind is over-tensioned.

Stopping a draught through a letterbox

Fit either a nylon brush letterbox draught excluder **(Cimco)** or a plastic flap **(Marley)** on the inside of the door over the aperture. (These items are available from hardware and department stores.) This will help stop the draught even if letters or a newspaper are left wedged in the opening.

Remember . . .

When working with broken glass, wear thick gloves to protect your hands.

Never use a blowlamp to remove paint from a window frame as the heat will crack the glass.

If paintwork is in good condition, it isn't always necessary to strip it off before repainting. Just rub it down well with wet or dry abrasive paper.

Before starting to paint doors or windows, remove all fitments such as handles, catches and doorplates. Any that cannot be removed should be masked carefully with newspaper or masking tape.

Always use *decorators'* masking tape. Ordinary self-adhesive tape is unsuitable because it doesn't peel off easily or neatly after use.

Windows and doors should not be painted when closed (unless the windows are the non-opening kind) or it may be impossible to open them after the paint has dried.

Always prime bare wood before painting with undercoat and a topcoat.

When easing casement windows that are stuck, do it carefully otherwise the frame may twist and shatter the glass.

Always fit safety glass into doors and windows that are in a vulnerable position, especially if children are likely to fall against them, such as French windows and front doors.

FLOORS AND FLOORING

Dealing with a damp concrete floor

If the problem is caused by rising damp you must have this cured professionally with a damp-proofing system such as the one offered by **Rentokil**. Once this has been done and the damp has receded you can lay any type of flooring.

If the dampness is not severe and is not caused by a structural problem, lay a floor covering like **Wicanders' Cork-O-Plast** which has a PVC foil layer on the underside to give extra protection against moisture. This is only suitable where the damp level is below **5%**—a builder will be able to check this for you with a moisture meter.

Making a neat join between two carpets

Cover the joins where carpets meet in doorways with aluminium strips such as **Cimco Edging Strips** from DIY shops and department stores.

Eliminating static shock from carpets

When you get a shock if you touch something metal after walking across carpet, it is due to the fact that most synthetic, and some natural, fibres cause an electrostatic charge to form with friction. This is aggravated by footwear, especially leather, and by dry conditions which are often caused by central heating.

The solution is to increase the humidity in carpeted rooms by keeping a fish tank, vases of flowers or bowls of water in the rooms.

Alternatively, you could buy a humidifier for each of the rooms. These can either be simply containers of water which can be hung on hot-water radiators, or are electrical devices which throw out a very fine moisture spray. Both have the effect of increasing the moisture in the air in the room. They are available from department stores and electrical shops.

Stopping rugs 'creeping' on carpets

Use **Antikreep** foam underlay stuck to the underside of the rug with **Copydex Adhesive** or a double-sided tape. **Antikreep** is available by the roll and in pre-cut sizes from carpet retailers. If you need to join two pieces together under a large rug, use **Copydex Carpet Binding Tape** with **Copydex Adhesive**. Alternatively, use **Copydex Double-Sided Adhesive Tape** stuck to the edges of the rug and the carpet underneath.

Do not stick **Antikreep** to the back of valuable Persian or Oriental rugs but just flop lay them on top of a piece cut to the correct size.

Eliminating ripples in carpets

These are often caused if you wet the carpet too much during shampooing or if a large quantity of water is spilled. This will either shrink or stretch it. The only solution is to have the carpet stretched professionally and to take care not to over-wet the carpet when you next shampoo.

Repairing a small burn in a carpet

You will need a spare piece of matching carpet and a small piece of hessian. With a sharp knife, cut out a neat section of carpet round the hole to remove any singed tufts. Cut a matching-sized piece from the spare carpet and a piece of hessian that is slightly larger. Slide the hessian into the hole and apply a carpet adhesive, such as **Copydex Adhesive**, round the edges so that the main piece of carpet sticks to it. Apply more adhesive to the carpet patch and place it in the hole so that the hessian holds it all together. With some carpets, you will need to check the direction of the pile before fitting the patch in place.

Fixing foam-backed carpet to vinyl flooring

To do this without damaging the vinyl tiles with nails or flooring adhesive, use **Copydex Double-Sided Adhesive Tape** which won't mark the vinyl and can be lifted without damaging it, even after the flooring has been down for some time.

First put down special grey paper felt (from carpet retailers) to prevent the foam backing sticking to the vinyl floor. Cut it slightly smaller than the room, leaving about 5 cm all the way round to allow for the tape. If the foam deteriorates and becomes sticky, the felt will prevent it damaging the tiles. Lay the carpet over the felt and cut it to size. Lay the double-sided tape round the edge of the room but do not peel off the top seal until you have fitted the carpet, then stick it down one side at a time. Gently pull the carpet as you stick it down to smooth out any slight ripples.

Raising flattened carpet pile

Where the pile of a carpet has been flattened by furniture, it is sometimes possible to raise it again by steaming. Lay a white cloth dampened with clean water over the area and press gently with a hot iron. When dry, brush up the pile of the carpet with a stiff brush.

Replacing an area of vinyl flooring

Worn or damaged patches of flooring can be dangerous as well as look unsightly. Patch them before there is an accident.

Mark around the hole with a pencil and, with a sharp knife, cut out the worn area neatly. Use a steel rule or piece of wood as a guide. Place the worn piece on the new vinyl and match up the pattern. Mark the outline on to the new piece and cut it to shape.

Clean the exposed floor to remove dust and any old adhesive. Apply a thin coat of **Evo-Stik Flooring Adhesive** to the back of the patch or fix double-sided tape all round the edge of the hole. Fix the patch in place, checking that the pattern matches, and tap it down flush with a flat piece of wood.

Removing indentations from cork tiles

If the damage is only slight, cork tiles can be sanded down with medium glasspaper. If the damage covers quite a large area, it might be wise to get a flooring contractor to do the job for you.

It is possible to replace damaged tiles but it is not an easy job and may result in damage to the surrounding tiles if great care is not taken. A flooring contractor will do the job for you if you prefer not to tackle it yourself.

To remove a badly damaged tile, first cut around the edges with a sharp knife, using a steel rule as a guide. With a chisel and mallet, prise the tile up, starting from a hole in the centre of the tile, so as not to damage the surrounding sound tiles. Scrape up any old adhesive and fit the new tile in position, trimming it slightly if necessary. Spread a thin layer of cork tile adhesive (available from DIY shops) on to the back of the new tile before pressing it firmly down into position.

Repairing cracked ceramic floor tiles

Carefully fill the cracks with an all-purpose filler, such as **Tetrion**. Leave to dry, then smooth over with glasspaper and tint it to match the rest of the tile, using a paint of similar colour carefully applied with a fine artist's paintbrush. For a perfect finish, employ a flooring contractor to cut out the broken tiles and replace them. Only do this when you are sure that matching replacement tiles can be obtained.

Restoring a damaged quarry tile floor

This is not an easy job so you may prefer to have it done by a professional flooring contractor.

To replace one damaged quarry tile, tap it with a cross-pein hammer so that the surface breaks up slightly. Working from the centre, chip out the broken pieces with a small cold chisel and a hammer. Wear goggles to protect your eyes from fragments. You will also need to chip out rough pieces on the concrete surface under the tile before laying the new tile. Check that the new tile fits and rests just below the surface of the other tiles before the adhesive is applied. Use a floor tile adhesive such as **Bal-Cem**. After 24 hours, grout the surrounding joints with **Bal-Grout** following the manufacturer's instructions.

If it is not possible to repair or replace your damaged quarry tiles, fill or screed the floor (see below) with **Marley Cement Mortar Screed Mix**, or get a flooring contractor to do the job for you. It will then be possible to cover the floor with any new floor covering.

Laying a levelling screed

This is necessary if you plan to lay a new floor over an uneven cement or damaged quarry tile floor.

If the floor has only a very few irregularities, fill these individually with an all-purpose filler such as **Tetrion**. Allow it to dry and sand lightly if necessary to render it level with the surrounding floor.

Large uneven areas need screeding all over. Use a compound such as **Marley Cement Mortar Screed Mix**, spread evenly and thinly over the floor with a float trowel. Very large areas are best screeded by a professional flooring contractor.

Filling gaps in floorboards

Use a filler such as **Joy Plastic Wood** or some papier mâché made from old newspaper torn into small squares and soaked in water overnight. Boil the soaked newspaper to a pulp and gradually add wallpaper paste or glue size in powder form until the mixture thickens. Fill the gaps firmly with either filler using a filling knife. Leave to dry and sand flush. This can be stained to match the floorboards with a wood stain.

Larger gaps should be filled with pieces of softwood planed into wedge shapes. Apply a PVA adhesive, such as **Evo-Stik Wood-working Adhesive**, to the softwood and knock the wedges into the gaps with a mallet. Plane and sand the wedges until flush and finish to match the rest of the floor.

Where gaps are very wide it is best to re-lay the floor. Replace worn boards with new ones of the same thickness and remember that you will need an extra one to fill the space that will be produced by closing up the small gaps. This will have to be sawn or planed down to fit into the remaining space.

Stopping stairs creaking

This is usually caused by the wedges or corner blocks working loose (see diagram). Hammer wedges back into position and refix corner blocks with a wood adhesive. Replace missing or damaged wedges with new ones made from timber offcuts. Apply **Evo-Stik Woodworking Adhesive** to them and hammer them into position.

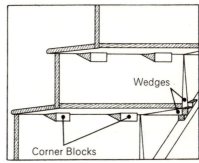

Wedges

Corner Blocks

Metal brackets can be fitted as an alternative to corner blocks. These are fixed in position with woodscrews.

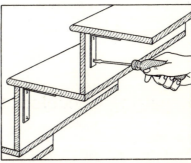

If the underside of your staircase is inaccessible, remove any stair covering and nail through the front of the tread into the riser. Drive the nail in at an angle and punch the head under. Replace the stair covering.

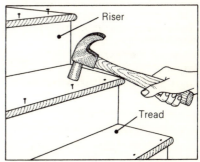

Riser

Tread

Stopping floorboards creaking

First, carefully remove any floor covering. With a claw hammer, remove any nails which have rusted, hammer down loose nails and punch down protruding nail heads. If you decide to put the nails into new positions, first check that in doing so you will not go through a water pipe or electric cable. Refix the boards to the joists with cut nails (from DIY shops and builders' merchants) hammered in at an angle. If you are likely to want to lift up the floorboards at a later date you should use countersunk woodscrews when fixing them down.

Staining plain floorboards

If the boards are damaged or already stained a dark colour, you will not be able to colour them effectively. Sand them down well first, then use a pigmented polyurethane varnish such as **Ronseal Woodshades**. The grain of the wood will show through the varnish. Alternatively, dye the cleaned boards with a stain such as **Rustins Matt Wood Stain** (in eight colours) and finish it with **Rustins Plastic Coating** to protect it and give it a shine.

Painting floorboards

For a coloured effect, you can paint floorboards with **Liquid Lino** which is semi-gloss and comes in ten colours plus black and white. It covers even dark wood but the boards must be unstained, dirt free and dry before you begin. Clean off wax and grime with steel wool moistened with white spirit. Heavily encrusted boards may need sanding. **Liquid Lino** will probably need repainting from time to time in heavy traffic areas.

Repairing woodblock floors

Woodblock floors are made up of individual squares or strips of hardwood glued together. Most have flush edges but some are tongued and grooved, ie one side of each block has a small projecting edge which fits neatly into a groove or recess on the next section of woodblock.

To repair a damaged block, first chisel out a small section from it, working from the centre. Remove the whole block and clean out the aperture. Check for fit with the new block. Spread wood glue over the exposed floor and press the new block into position, tapping it flush with a mallet to avoid damaging it. A replacement tongue-and-groove block should have the lower edge of the groove cut off so that it can easily be fixed into place.

Remember . . .

Although quarry-tile flooring looks good, it is cold and hard to stand on for long periods of time, and old, worn quarry tiles can be difficult to clean and maintain.

When working on floors in upstairs rooms, take care not to hammer too hard as the extra vibration may crack ceilings below.

Before laying a new floor covering, secure any loose boards and punch down any protruding nail heads.

Never lay new floor covering over an uneven or damp floor. Correct the problems at their source first.

If you are not sure how to calculate the amount of flooring needed, make a sketch of the room, with the measurements on it, and take this to the shop.

It is better to replace a section of damaged floorboard than to repair it.

When buying and laying new stair carpet, allow for some extra length so it can be moved every year or so (depending on use) to even out wear.

KITCHENS AND BATHROOMS

Repairing a cracked washbasin

You must replace any washbasin with a crack in it, but a temporary repair can be effected by glueing strips of linen (old sheets or pillow-cases) to the outside of the crack with **Bostik 1 Clear Adhesive** and painting them white. An alternative and probably longer-lasting repair can be made by spreading **Isopon Polyester Repair Paste** over the crack and leaving it to dry.

Curing a leaking loo

This usually occurs when the compound joint between the loo and the outlet pipe breaks. You need a special cement, such as **Blue Hawk Quick-Setting Cement** (from DIY shops), which works fast even on wet surfaces.

Clean the area round the leak and rake out any loose debris. Put polythene sheeting on the floor round the loo and bail out as much water as possible. Make up the cement following the instructions and use a trowel or scraper to press it into the joint. Smooth it off and leave to dry for about 30 minutes before using the loo again.

Unblocking a loo

You need a special plunger, slightly larger than a sink plunger and fitted with a metal rim round the edge to prevent it from turning inside-out. Buy one at a builders' merchant.

Push this plunger as far as possible down into the pan and work it up and down several times very quickly. Be careful not to scratch the pan with the metal rim of the plunger. If this does not succeed in shifting the blockage you will need to call a plumber.

If you do not have a plunger, small blockages, such as too much loo paper pushed into the loo by children, can sometimes be cleared by pushing a long piece of springy wire (like that used for hanging net curtains) round the U bend.

Unblocking a sink

Try a proprietary drain cleaner or a cupful of washing soda dissolved in hot water. Some drain cleaners are caustic, so use with great care following the manufacturer's directions. Alternatively, use a sink plunger (from hardware shops or builders' merchants). Block off the sink overflow, remove all but about 3 cm of water from the sink and work the plunger vigorously up and down over the outlet. Take care to be more gentle with a washbasin or you may loosen the wall brackets.

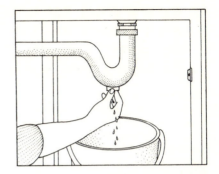

If this does not work, tackle the U bend. Place a bucket underneath it to protect the floor and carefully remove the screw plug and washer at the bottom of the bend. Loosen it first with an adjustable spanner, then unscrew it by hand. Push a piece of flexible wire (curtain wire is ideal) down the sink outlet and, using a twisting action, work the wire up and down to loosen the blockage.

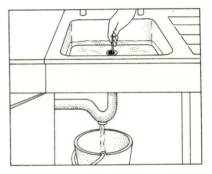

If the blockage won't budge, push the wire up through the U bend into the section of pipe which leads away from the bend.

Flush through with water and then replace the screw plug, checking that it's watertight. (Keep a bucket under the trap.) If you have a modern plastic trap without a plug, unscrew the waste section at the bottom of the trap (you'll need a large adjustable spanner). Take careful note of where washers were fitted, and replace them if necessary.

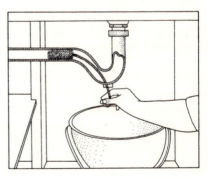

Unblocking an aerosol

Carefully remove the button from the top of the aerosol by pulling it upwards. Wash the button in a solution of washing-up liquid and rinse. Clear the hole with a fine sewing needle. Holding the container with the spray directed away from you, push the button gently back on to the valve stem and rotate until the hole is in the correct position.

Stopping a loo cistern overflowing

Flow into the loo cistern is controlled by a ball valve fixed to an arm and ball float. As the float rises with the water level, it causes a piston to close a valve and stop any more water flowing into the cistern. An overflow can be caused by the float arm being too high.

Turn off the supply to the cistern and carefully bend the ball arm down, using an adjustable spanner near the ball end. Aim to move the arm by about one or two centimetres. If the fault persists, check the ball which may have become corroded or split. If so, unscrew it and replace it with a new plastic one (from DIY and hardware shops).

A further reason for an overflow may be that the washer on the valve needs replacing. If your cistern has the old type of valve, remove the split pin, which connects the arm of the ball float to the piston, with a pair of pliers. Remove the piston from its housing by pushing the tip of a screwdriver up through a slot in the underneath. Clean the piston with fine steel wool. To unscrew the end cap, insert the screwdriver in the slot in the side of the piston and hold the cap in a pair of pliers while turning the piston. Remove the rubber washer which is probably worn or perished. Fit a new washer, which can be bought from builders' merchants or DIY shops. Take the old washer with you as a sample when buying a replacement. Replace the piston and refit the split pin into the arm and valve assembly. Turn on the water supply and check that no further overflowing occurs.

If you have the more modern type of valve, all you need do is unscrew the end cap with a pair of pliers and fit a new diaphragm (from DIY and hardware shops). Reassemble the valve and tighten up the screw cap.

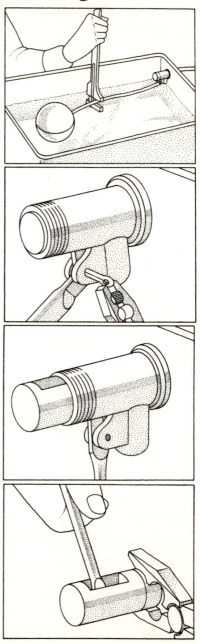

Replacing damaged ceramic tiles

Provided only one or two tiles are damaged or cracked, it is more sensible to replace them than to retile the whole area. Check first that you have or can obtain matching replacement tiles.

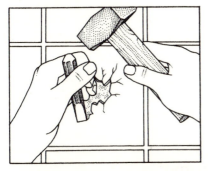

Wear goggles to protect your eyes and, using a small cold chisel and hammer, carefully crack the damaged tile into small bits. Work outwards from the centre of each tile. Remove all the pieces and scrape out old adhesive and grouting. Check that the base on which you will stick the new tile is flat.

Test fit the tile into the gap to make sure it will lie horizontally and vertically in line. If not, build a support from matchsticks held in place with self-adhesive tape (**Sellotape**) to hold the position. You will be able to fill uneven gaps between tiles with grouting.

Apply **Bal-Wall Ceramic Tile Adhesive** with a notched spreader to the back of each tile, fixing one before you apply adhesive to the next. Press the tile into position and wipe off surplus adhesive with a damp cloth. When all the new tiles are in position, leave them for 24 hours to allow the adhesive to set hard before removing any match-sticks. Grout between the tiles following the manufacturer's instructions. An extra layer of grouting applied over both old and new tiles will give the whole area a better finish (see page 40).

Drilling into ceramic tiles

Drilling into a ceramic surface is a more effective way of fixing fitments than using double-sided self-adhesive tabs. The important thing is to stop the drill sliding about on the tile and cracking it.

Stick masking tape over the area you are drilling and mark the points where you are going to make the holes. Use the slowest speed to prevent the bit overheating and to ensure an accurate cut. When you have drilled the appropriate-sized hole, remove the tape, plug the hole and screw in the fitment.

Tiling over existing tiles

Replacing crazed or unattractive tiling can involve a lot of replastering and other work which could be avoided by simply covering the old tiles with new ceramic tiles, such as **Johnson's Cristal**.

A cheaper alternative is to stencil over the tiles. Make up a cardboard stencil and spray or brush on paint. This solution is not very durable but is a good temporary measure, and may help to brighten up a bathroom.

Renewing grouting between tiles

After a period of time, the grouting between tiles becomes dirty and crumbly and, if cleaning with a domestic bleach solution has ceased to work, you will need to renew it. Regrouting improves the appearance of a tiled area enormously.

With an old chisel or screwdriver, scrape out all the old grout from between the tiles. Using a rubber-bladed spreader (a window-cleaning device works well), apply the new grout. Wipe off the surplus and allow it to dry. Finish off by polishing the tiles with a soft cloth. If the tiles are thick you may need to apply a second layer to get a flush finish.

If you are regrouting a tiled worktop, use an impervious grouting material which is stain resistant to avoid having to repeat the job frequently. **Bal-Epoxy Grout** is available from DIY shops and builders' merchants—write for a local stockist to Building Adhesives Ltd, Longton Road, Trentham, Stoke-on-Trent, Staffs.

When renewing grouting, it is possible to add a colour pigment, such as **Bal-Grout Colour Mix** to the grouting to match the colour of the tiles.

Making a ceramic worktop

For the base, use blockboard which is strong and won't sag under the weight of the tiles. If you are making a worktop to fit across a long unsupported span, you may need to insert a support or reinforce the unit underneath with a batten along the length of the new worktop. Choose DIY tiles from a range such as **H & R Johnson's** and stick them on to the blockboard with a tile adhesive. Grout when dry (see above).

Remember, when tiling an area such as a worktop, to plan the tile positions before applying any adhesive. Ensure the tiles are square and that you have taken the spacing between them into consideration when doing your calculations. If the length of the worktop is not fixed, it's best to lay the tiles out first and mark the corners with a pencil. If you need to saw the wood or plane any edges, do so before the tiles are stuck down.

When buying tiles, remember that some may need cutting. Some shops will do this for you if you provide them with precise measurements, but this will cost extra, of course.

Sealing a gap between bath and wall

A gap between a bath and the wall can allow water to seep through to the ceiling of the room below (especially if you have an over-bath shower). Use a mastic such as **Evo-Stik Colourseal** which comes in white, green, yellow, pink, blue and beige to match British Standard sanitaryware colours. The tube has a nozzle applicator which makes it possible to achieve a neat, smooth seal which adheres firmly to both surfaces but is flexible enough when dry to allow for slight movement when the bath is used. It dries with a porcelain-like gloss which blends well with both the bath and the surrounding ceramic tiles.

Bridging a gap between worktop and wall

Small gaps of this kind give an unfinished appearance and act as dirt traps. Cover them with plastic or wood beading which is available in various sizes from DIY shops and timber yards.

Stick the beadings with a contact adhesive, such as **Bostik 3**, or use panel pins with wood which can then be painted or varnished.

Putting new worktops on old units

Make your own by buying a section of blockboard or chipboard and sticking on a laminated plastic of your choice. Alternatively, ready-made worktops are usually available in 3-m lengths from timber yards, or you can order them by the metre from kitchen showrooms or builders' merchants.

Repairing chipped melamine surfaces

Fill the chipped area with plastic wood or **Interior Polyfilla** and when dry smooth it to shape with fine glasspaper. Apply **Humbrol Enamel** in a similar colour or use a mixture of colours to give an approximate colour match.

Removing black mould from sealant between bath and wall

Use an old clean toothbrush dipped in neat domestic bleach to scrub the stained areas. Take care not to splash bleach either on yourself or the surrounding areas. Rinse well with clear water and wipe dry. Alternatively, use a bactericide such as **Fungo** (available from Dax Products Ltd, 76 Cyprus Road, Nottingham, if you cannot get it at your local hardware shop), following the manufacturer's instructions.

Protect the surrounding floor and any shower curtains, and wear an overall and household gloves with either of these treatments.

Renewing a damaged non-stick pan

It is not possible to do this effectively yourself and, in general, pan manufacturers do not offer a re-coating service.

A flaking non-stick lining is not a health hazard but will affect the properties of the pan and you may prefer to remove the whole surface.

Use a **Scotchbrite** pad or fine gauge steel wool moistened with water to remove the coating. Wear gloves to protect your hands.

Replacing a tap washer

Turn off the water supply to the tap and unscrew the chrome cover. If this is tight use an adjustable spanner with a piece of cloth between its jaws to protect the chrome. Turn the tap on to its fullest extent and raise the chrome cover. This will reveal the large hexagonal nut that screws into the base and holds the working parts together.

If the tap has a plastic top it will be held in position with a retaining screw under a plastic button. Prise of the button, loosen the screw, remove it and pull the plastic top upwards and off.

Use an adjustable spanner to undo the large hexagonal nut. Hold the tap steady with your other hand while you apply pressure with the spanner.

Remove the jumper (the part that holds the washer) and unscrew the retaining nut that holds the washer in place. Use a pair of pliers and a spanner to do this.

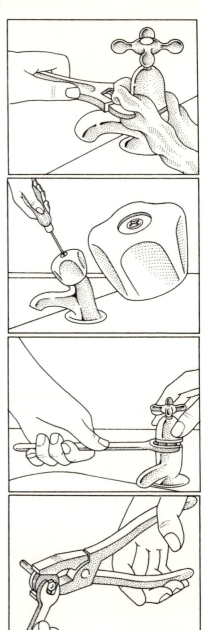

Replace the worn washer with a new one of the same size. Refit the jumper and reassemble the tap by reversing the process. Turn on the water supply again.

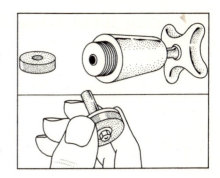

Replacing a washer on a Supatap

There is no need to turn off the water supply when replacing a washer in a Supatap. Turn the tap slightly on and use an adjustable spanner to unscrew the large hexagonal nut at the top of the nozzle. Unscrew the nozzle to remove it. The water flow will stop as you do this.

Press down on the tip of the nozzle to free the anti-splash device which is situated at the bottom of it. The tip of the device is just visible inside the nozzle. Alternatively, push the device out from the top of the nozzle with a pencil or screwdriver.

Use a screwdriver to lever the washer jumper out of the anti-splash device and replace it with a new one (from builders' merchants and DIY shops). Replace the washer-jumper in the anti-splash device and drop this back into the nozzle. Screw the nozzle back on to the tap and tighten up the hexagonal nut. Turn the tap off completely.

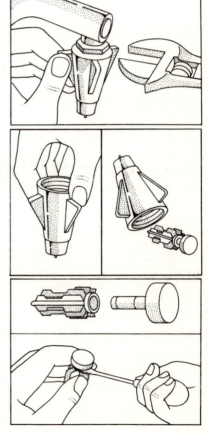

Repairing damaged tap heads

If an acrylic knob on a tap breaks, try to repair it with a super glue such as **Bostik 12**. If this doesn't work replace both tap heads with the **Opella Tap Converson Set** or **Mr. Plumber Tap Converters** from DIY shops and builders' merchants. Unscrew the old tap mechanism, cover and top, and fit the new one in its place. Make sure you put the correct head on the hot and cold taps.

Repairing a chipped enamel bath

It is not possible to make an invisible repair but **Joy Porcelainit** should make it look less unsightly. Chipped areas likely to be exposed to hot water should be filled with **David's Isopon Polyester Repair Paste**.

Clean the area thoroughly to remove grease and soap deposits and dry well. Mix the paste according to the instructions and fill in the chips just proud of the surrounding surface. After about 10 minutes they should be dry enough for you to smooth the repairs down with medium glasspaper. Paint to match the bath as near as possible with an enamel paint such as **Joy** or **Humbrol**.

Removing scratches from a plastic bath

Use a metal polish such as **Silvo** to remove light scratches. Deeper scratches will need rubbing out with a fine emery cloth (from DIY or hardware shops) followed by an application of metal polish, buffed well to restore the surface shine.

Improving damaged laminate surfaces

This is virtually impossible since although laminates are tough they are susceptible to heat and scratching. It is sometimes possible to burnish out slight marks by using a fine steel wool pad and then polishing the surface with a spray on furniture polish, but this is not a good idea for surfaces where food is prepared. In general, it is best to renew a badly marked laminate surface and then look after it.

Formica has produced a useful booklet called *How to care for Formica laminate* which is free from Formica Ltd, 99 Kensington High Street, London W8. Send a stamped addressed envelope for your copy.

De-furring a shower spray nozzle

Unscrew the metal nozzle from the pipe, using pipe grips if it is stiff from scale build-up. Protect the chrome with a piece of cloth round the grips. Lay the spray nozzle in a shallow container and pour **Descalite** descaler (made up according to the instructions) over it. If it is heavily scaled, use a thin metal skewer or thick needle to clean the holes individually. Rinse thoroughly in clean water before reassembling.

De-furring an electric kettle

In hard-water areas, a coating of chalk—known as furring—can develop inside a kettle. A furred-up kettle is less efficient and costs more to use than it should. Check on the kettle manufacturer's instructions to see if a special product is required. If not, buy **Albright Scale Away** or **Descalite** descaler (from hardware shops, department stores and some chemists) and follow the instructions on the packet. Badly scaled kettles may need two treatments. Be sure to follow the maker's instructions for neutralising the descaler before using the kettle.

Replacing a broken loo seat

A broken loo seat must be replaced with a new seat and lid. When buying a new loo seat, take the measurement of the fixings at the back and the distance between them with you to make sure you get the correct type of seat for your loo.

To fit the new seat, remove the old bolts holding the fixing assembly. If these are corroded, spray with an aerosol lubricant such as **Rocket WD40**. Fix the new seat according to the instructions supplied with it.

Repairing buffers on the underneath of a loo seat

These can be refixed with a clear adhesive such as **Bostik 1** or **UHU**. If the buffers are beyond repair, your local building material suppliers should be able to order new ones for you, provided you know the make of the seat. If not, it will be necessary to buy a new seat.

Remember . . .

When putting up new ceramic wall tiles, it is not necessary to remove old ones which are in reasonably good condition—you can tile over them (see page 39).

Always turn water off at the mains when replacing tap washers or working on water cisterns.

Use dust sheets to protect bath and basin from damage when working in the bathroom.

There are strict Bye-laws on water usage and permitted fitments, so check with your local water authority before carrying out any DIY plumbing installations.

Take care not to apply too much pressure when using a plunger to unblock a loo, sink or washbasin as this may loosen the fitment and joints and cause leaks.

After de-furring a kettle or coffee maker be sure to neutralise the chemicals used. Follow the directions given with the de-furring product before using the appliances to prepare drinks.

Do not attempt to paint a laminated work surface in a kitchen. The finish will not be durable enough to withstand general use, and chips of paint could get into food.

FURNITURE

Replacing a damaged piece of veneer

You will need to remove the damaged piece and replace it. New veneer can be bought at DIY and art shops.

Soften the damaged section by leaving a piece of dampened cotton wool over it for some hours. Lay a piece of new veneer over the section, taking care to match the direction of the grain. With a craft or **Stanley** knife, cut through both thicknesses of veneer so that the new piece is an exact copy of the damaged section underneath.

Remove the damaged piece and clean out the old glue from the hole with a narrow-bladed chisel. Take care not to damage the veneer on either side of the piece you are replacing.

Check that the new piece of veneer is not too thin or too thick. If it is too thin, use an extra piece of veneer; if too thick, sand down the underneath of the piece until it lies flush with the existing veneered surface.

Wet the new piece of veneer so that it is pliable. Apply an adhesive, eg **Evo-Stik Woodworking Adhesive**, to the bare surfaces and fit the new section in. Press it into position and wipe off any excess adhesive. Use a screwdriver handle to roll the seam so that the edges are stuck down firmly. Clamp or put weights on it until the adhesive is dry.

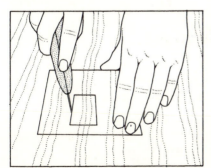

Repairing blistered veneer

Slice through the blister with a sharp craft knife such as a **Plasplugs** or **Stanley**. Place a piece of damp cotton wool over the damaged section and leave it undisturbed for a couple of hours.

Remove the cotton wool and check if the veneer has softened enough with the moisture to become pliable.

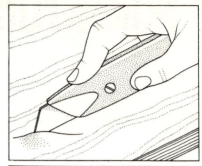

Carefully extend the slit to loosen a greater area so that the adhesive can make a firmer join. Gently apply a wood glue, such as **Bostik 8 PVA**, under the surface with the blade of a flat knife or a needle if the cut is very small. Flatten the veneer with your fingers and wipe away any surplus glue.

Hold in position with a clamp, pile of weights or heavy books. Put a piece of greaseproof paper between the repair and the weights to stop them sticking together.

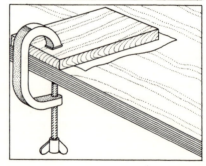

Removing small dents from a wooden surface

With white spirit, wipe off the polish on the damaged area. Place a piece of dampened cotton wool over the dent and leave for a few hours. When the wood has swelled to the level of the rest of the surrounding surface, remove the cotton wool.

On solid wood you can, as an alternative method, use a piece of wet blotting paper under the tip of a warm iron to raise the dent. Let the wood dry thoroughly before you repolish the repair.

Repairing deep dents in a table top

Deep dents will not respond to softening with moisture. Use a wood filler such as **Brummer Stopping** which comes in various wood shades such as mahogany, oak, etc. Press the filler into the dent with a filling knife, starting with a small quantity and building up until it is level with the surface. Let each layer dry before applying the next. Smooth off with fine glasspaper and polish as usual.

Covering a scratch on a polished surface

Fill fine scratches with a very little matching shoe polish applied with a matchstick, then polish as usual.

Deeper scratches can be filled by rubbing a wax crayon over them or by filling with melted beeswax coloured to match with a wood stain. Take care not to polish them too hard or too often as these remedies do not make a durable finish.

Restoring a faded section on a table

Folding tables can become more faded on the centre section because of exposure to sunlight. If the colour of the wood has faded, it is difficult to restore, but if it is the polish that has faded and lost its shine, try using **Colron Restorer and Cleaner** on the surface. Polish with your usual cream or **Colron Liquid Wax** afterwards.

Removing a build-up of wax

Use white spirit applied a little at a time on a soft cloth. Mop up the loosened wax and dirt as you go. You may need more than one application to remove a heavy build-up. *Note that white spirit is flammable.*

With valuable and antique furniture, use **Colron Restorer and Cleaner**. This will remove the soiled build-up but not the patina created by years of polishing.

Removing a smell of mothballs

While mothballs protect the contents of drawers and cupboards, their distinctive odour can be difficult to eradicate. With drawers, first turn them upside down and bang the base to loosen fluff and dirt. Then wipe out drawers or cupboard interiors with a cloth wrung out in a hot solution of washing-up liquid. Rinse with a cloth dampened with a weak disinfectant solution and leave to dry naturally with the drawers out of their housing and the cupboard doors open.

If any smell of mothballs lingers, two or three drops of vanilla essence dripped along the joins inside drawers or cupboards should counteract it.

Strengthening wobbly table legs

If a joint has come clean apart, scrape out the old adhesive and restick with **Evo-Stik Woodworking Adhesive**. Very loose joints can be strengthened with a bracket and/or screws to restore their angle and strength.

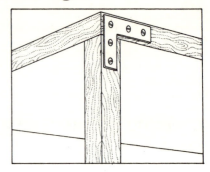

Refixing a damaged table top

Many table tops are made up of more than one section of wood and these, with time and use, can come unstuck and start to move apart. Before sticking them back together, clean off all the old adhesive from the table-top edges, using a scraper and medium glasspaper.

Apply **Evo-Stik** or other PVA woodworking adhesive along both of the edges being glued together. Use two battens and wedges to make a clamp—screw the battens to a workbench or piece of solid wood. Lay the table-top sections between the battens and fix in the wedges to hold the wood firmly. Wipe off any surplus glue.

For extra strength, before you remove the clamp, fix two or three flat

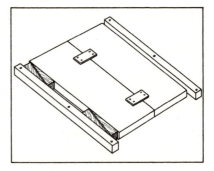

metal jointing plates across the join on the underside of the table top. Pre-drill the screw holes and use short wood screws which won't go through and be visible on the surface of the table.

Repairing a folding (gate-leg) table

If the leaves of a folding table sag when raised into position, this can be caused by strain on old hinges. Replacing them with new ones should solve the problem. An easier solution is to cut a sliver of wood and

to glue and pin it to the underside of the leaf so that it lies above the gate leg supporting the leaf when it is in the 'up' position. Use a woodworking adhesive such as **Evo-Stick Woodworking Adhesive**.

Repairing a rickety dining chair

Loose or missing corner blocks which should hold the legs of the chair firm and the seat in place, are often found to be the cause of a rickety chair.

If the chair has an upholstered and sprung seat, you need to remove the base hessian cover to get at the corner blocks. If it has a loose upholstered seat, all you need to do is lift the seat out.

Tighten up the screws holding the corner blocks in place. If the blocks are very loose, re-glue them into position with a wood glue, eg **Evo-Stik Woodworking Adhesive**, before tightening up the screws. If any of

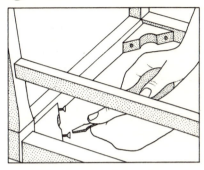

the blocks are missing, you can make new ones from off-cuts of wood, making use of the existing ones as a pattern.

Strengthening chair legs

When a chair starts to wobble, strengthen it by fixing metal angle brackets into the corners formed by the legs and the underside of the seat frame.

First clamp the chair into the correct position using a **Stanley Web Clamp** or a home-made string

tourniquet made by looping a piece of string round two of the legs and twisting it with a small batten until it pulls the legs into position. Fix the brackets in place with wood screws and when you have tightened them release the clamp.

Mending a broken chair rail

With *square* or *oblong* rails you can effect a repair by fixing a metal plate at the back and on the underside of the rails to hold the two sections together. Camouflage the plates with a coat of paint. However, do bear in mind that the repaired chair will not be as strong as it was originally so treat it with care.

A *round* rail, or a square one which is broken in two places, cannot be repaired with metal plates and needs to be replaced. Cut out the old rail with a tenon saw and thoroughly clean out the housing at either end

with a chisel.

Buy a new piece of wood the same dimension as the original rail and plane it into shape if necessary. Measure the size of the housings carefully and cut the ends of the new rail to form joints that will fit tightly. Apply a woodworking glue, such as **Evo-Stik Woodworking Adhesive**, to the holes and pull the chair slightly apart so that the new rail can be inserted. Wipe off surplus glue and apply a clamp or string tourniquet (see above) to the chair to hold the repair in position until dry.

Replacing drawer knobs

Wooden knobs on old furniture often work loose, come off and get mislaid. You can buy a wide variety of replacement knobs from DIY shops and specialists such as **Knobs and Knockers** (see page 119, mail order service available).

Fill the hole where the original knob was fitted with a piece of dowel glued into position. With a small tenon saw, cut the protruding end flush with the surface. (Place a template of thin card over the front of the drawer or cupboard to prevent the saw marking it.)

When the glue is thoroughly dry place the drawer on a firm surface. With a hand drill (so you have greater control) make a hole of the right diameter for the bolt of the new knob. Fit the knob and tighten up the nut and bolt on the inside of the drawer.

Easing sticking drawers

First rub along the runners with glasspaper and then with a piece of soap or a candle. If the drawer still sticks, it may be because slight damp or condensation has caused the wood to swell. Use a **Surform** shaper to remove thin shavings from the areas that are sticking and, for good measure, apply soap or candle wax before putting the drawer back.

Replacing worn drawer runners

Where the drawer runners are simply extensions of the drawer's sides they can become worn, especially when the drawer is loaded with heavy items. To replace them you must first plane down the worn runners until they are level all along their length. Use a rasp or glasspaper when you get to the ends at the front of the drawer as the plane will not be able to reach into the angle. Do not cut the front of the drawer.

Glue a thin piece of hardwood on to each side and plane to shape if necessary. Sand the edges of the new sections with glasspaper and rub soap or a candle along them to make them run smoothly.

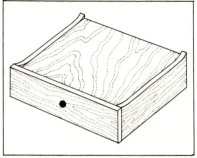

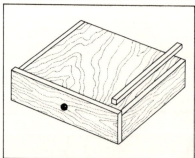

Repairing a broken drawer

Where the joints of a drawer have broken and cannot be repaired, use small brass brackets inside all four corners. Fix them with short screws that will not protrude through to the outside of the drawer. If the drawers are deep, you may need more than one bracket at each corner.

Repairing a drawer base

When the base of a slotted construction drawer is damaged, it is fairly simple to slide it out and insert a new one. Pull out any panel pins fixing the base to the sides, slide out the old base and clean out the recesses. Apply woodworking adhesive, eg **Evo-Stik**, to the recesses and slide in the new base section. Wipe off surplus glue and allow to dry before placing the drawer back in its casing.

When the base and sides on a fixed construction drawer have come apart you can reinforce the joint with 6-mm quadrant beading. Attach the beading inside the drawer along the bottom edges of the sides using panel pins and woodworking adhesive. Wipe off surplus glue and allow to dry before putting the drawer back into position.

Repairing old-fashioned castors

Brass castors If brass castors have become stiff, cleaning and oiling them will help them to move more freely. Take care to wipe off any surplus oil so it won't mark the floor.

If the screws holding the castors to the legs or base of furniture have worked loose, take them out. Fill the worn screw holes by glueing in a matchstick or sliver of wood and replace the screws.˙

Swivel castors When swivel castors become worn, the wheel starts to buckle under the weight of the furniture. Tighten up the shaft holding the castor assembly by tapping it lightly with a hammer and centre punch. Support the castor while doing this to avoid strain on the wheel section.

Broken castor spindles Replace a broken castor spindle with a nail. If there is an old piece of spindle inside the castor, punch it out with a nail and hammer. Push a new nail through and cut off the protruding length with a small hacksaw. Knock the end of the nail over with a hammer to spread the metal and prevent it falling out. This should make the castor run freely again.

Replacing a piano key cover

First scrape any remaining adhesive off the top of the key and the underside of the cover. Make sure it is free of dust.

Use a clear adhesive such as **UHU** or **Bostik 1 Clear**. Apply it sparingly to the top of the key taking care not to let it drip down the sides or spread on to other keys. Press the cover back into position and do not play the piano until the glue has dried. This repair should stand up to hard wear.

Painting cane furniture

To get a first-class finish you need to prepare cane funiture carefully. If it has been painted beforehand you must strip off all the old paint before applying the new. Wipe the cane thoroughly to ensure that it is free of dust, grease and moisture before you start painting.

An aerosol such as **Holts Handy Spray Gloss Paint** will give the best finish and does not require an undercoat. Cover all nearby surfaces with newspaper secured with sticky tape where necessary, and mask off any parts of the furniture, such as knobs and handles, which are not going to be painted. Hold the aerosol about 15 cm away from the cane and spray, using a gentle stroking movement and working in small sections. Start and finish each movement just beyond the area you want to cover. Remember that several light coats are better than one heavy one which may result in the paint 'sagging'.

If you are going to paint the cane with a brush, you will first need to rub it over lightly with glasspaper to give a good adhesive surface, and you will need both an undercoat and a topcoat. A paint with a polyurethane base such as **Crown Plus Two Non-Drip Full Gloss** will give the best finish.

Mending a tear in vinyl upholstery

A clean slit or tear in vinyl upholstery should be mended from the back. Cut a piece of vinyl material larger than the length of the tear that is as near a match as possible. Coat it with **Copydex**, gently lift one side of the slit with a knitting needle and slide it into position. Press the edges of the slit together and hold them there for a few minutes until the adhesive starts to grip. Alternatively, use **PVX Plastic Sealer**. Follow the manufacturer's instructions.

Holes should also be patched from the back if possible, using the same method. If this is not possible, stick a patch on top. Apply **Copydex** round the edge of the patch and the edge of the hole and leave until nearly dry before pressing them together.

Small tears and holes such as cigarette burns can be repaired with an **Instant Leather-Look Repair Kit** made by **Vinylize Systems**. This comes with a number of different coloured pastes so you can get a very good match. You bond the paste to the vinyl using an iron. Fabric pattern moulds are supplied so that you can imprint a matching grain on to the repaired section. The kit is available from most hardware shops.

Re-sticking a leather desk top

Carefully lift any loose corners or edges and scrape away the old dried adhesive from underneath with a knife. Make sure it is all removed from both the underside of the leather and the desk top.

Apply a thin coat of contact adhesive such as **Evo-Stik Impact** to both surfaces and let it dry for the recommended time—about 5–10 minutes. Working towards the corner, smooth the leather into position and press down. A weight, such as a pile of books, can be left on top overnight.

Disguising scratch marks on leather upholstery

Moisten along the exposed grain with a finger dipped in water. Push the surface of the leather back into its original position using your fingernail. Allow the section to dry for about 30 minutes then touch it up with a matching shade of **Connolly Coloured Lacquer**. This can be obtained by sending a tiny off-cut of the original (removed from an inconspicuous area, making sure the off-cut matches the scratched area which may have faded) together with your request to Connolly Bros (Curriers) Ltd, Wandle Bank, Wimbledon, London SW19 1DW. They will send a pro forma invoice stating carriage and price of the product and, on receipt of payment, will arrange for the product to be delivered. This lacquer takes only 2–3 minutes to dry, after which the scratch should be invisible.

Remember . . .

Never attempt to renovate antique or valuable furniture yourself as you could affect its appearance and value.

Never attempt repairs to large items unless you have plenty of space to work in.

Many proprietary products used for furniture repairs are toxic and give off fumes. Make sure you use them correctly, in a well ventilated room. Do not smoke and follow the manufacturers' directions carefully.

When reglueing wooden sections of a piece of furniture, remove all traces of old glue first. Use a scraper or rasp to get rid of the build-up.

When clamping reglued items together while the adhesive dries, always put cardboard or pieces of rag between the jaws of the clamp to protect the repaired item.

Never re-use old woodscrews as the heads will be worn and they will be difficult to drive in.

A little soap or wax candle rubbed on to the thread of a woodscrew will make it easier to tighten up.

It is much cheaper to re-upholster, or simply to re-cover, dining chairs or three-piece suites than to buy new ones, and re-upholstering can make the oldest furniture look almost like new.

CHINA, GLASS AND TABLEWARE

Mending the chipped rim of a plate

Sylglas Make or Break Kit should enable you to make a near invisible repair. Mix the two putties in the kit and fill the chipped area. When dry, rub it down with fine glasspaper and reglaze with the glazing substance provided. Bake it in the oven at 160°C (325°F) mark 3 to harden the glaze, having first checked with the manufacturer that the plate will stand this temperature. Note that if the plate is white there may be a slight colour change as white is difficult to match exactly.

The kit also includes an adhesive (for replacing broken sections), pigments and thinners (for brush-cleaning, etc.) so that you can paint the repaired area to match the surround before glazing. With practice it is possible to achieve a good match and finish.

Refixing a knife handle

Provided that neither the handle nor the tang at the base of the knife blade is broken, it is possible to refix the two together securely.

Rake out all the old fixing material from inside the handle using a thin screwdriver or metal skewer. Take care not to exert too much pressure or the handle may split. Remove any old glue with warm water and leave the handle to dry thoroughly before refixing. Gently clean the tang with a file or glasspaper until the bare metal shows all the way along.

Partially fill the hole in the handle with an epoxy resin adhesive, eg **Araldite Rapid**, or a bonding paste, eg **Plastic Padding**. Using a metal skewer, work the glue down into the handle until it is about half full.

Slowly push the tang into the handle, working it gently from side to side so that the glue is spread around the tang. Make sure the handle ends up in the correct position.

Wipe off any surplus glue that has bubbled out of the handle with a damp cloth. Bind around the join with adhesive tape **(Sellotape)**. Stand the knife blade-down in a jam jar and leave the adhesive to harden. Remove the adhesive tape and carefully scrape off any adhesive still on the blade or handle.

Sharpening a carving knife

All kitchen knives need regular sharpening to keep them working efficiently. In general, saw-edged blades need professional sharpening but knives with a continuous cutting edge or hollow-ground blade can be done at home with a sharpening steel, flat oil stone, hand-operated sharpener or electric sharpening machine. With practice, it is possible to sharpen scallop-edged blades with a hand-operated sharpener.

Sharpening steel When using a steel, hold the knife in your left hand (unless you are left-handed) with the sharp edge to the right. Cross the blades of the knife and steel at right angles close to the handles. Turn the knife so that the flat of the blade is at an angle of 30° to the steel and press the blades together. Slide the steel down the blade and repeat on the other side of the knife blade. Do this several times until the knife is sharp.

Rinse both knife and steel before cutting food.

Oil stone Before using a flat stone, cover it with a light oil such as **3-in-One**. Hold the knife at an angle of about 30° to the stone and rub it gently over the surface, keeping it moving so that the whole knife edge is worked on. When you have raised a roughened edge on the knife blade turn it over and rub gently along the stone to smooth it off.

Hand sharpener or electric sharpening machine When using either of these to sharpen a knife, follow the manufacturer's instructions.

Check if a knife blade is correctly sharpened all along its length by looking for a line of light reflected from the cutting edge. Where the line is broken or uneven you can detect the blunt patches.

Mending an alabaster ashtray or ornament

Use **Bostik 1 Clear Adhesive** or **Bostik 7 Epoxy Resin Adhesive** following the instructions.

Take special care not to get any adhesive on the alabaster except on the broken surfaces. Alabaster should never be immersed in water and any accidentally spilled adhesive should be wiped off immediately with a damp cloth.

Sticking a handle back on a cup

Cups that you often use and therefore wash up regularly should have their handles stuck back on with an epoxy resin adhesive such as **Araldite Rapid** or **Bostik 7**. Cups that live in a display cabinet can be repaired almost invisibly with **Bostik 1 Clear Adhesive**.

Mending chips in glassware

This requires specialist treatment from a professional. It is expensive, so it is only really worth having it done on valuable pieces of glass.

Two firms offering the service are: Ashton Bostock China Repairs and Thomas Goode & Co. Ltd (see page 119).

Remember . . .

Repairing china can work out costly if you have to buy an expensive adhesive. It's not worth repairing everyday items which can be replaced cheaply.

When sending items away for repair, be sure they are packed properly and insured in case of loss. Remember to take this into account when estimating the cost of the repair as it might affect your decision to have the repair done.

Take care when using a cup or jug with a reglued handle. Although modern adhesives make strong repairs, it is possible that handles may be weakened by repair, and the heat produced by washing them in a dishwasher could affect the strength of the repair.

Dirty china can be difficult to repair. Make sure it is absolutely clean and dry before dealing with it. A little denture cleaner will get difficult stains off but make sure all traces are rinsed off and the items dried before repairs are carried out.

Use **Plasticine** or **Bostik Blu Tack** to support small, awkwardly-shaped objects while they dry after glueing.

Make sure excess adhesive is wiped off immediately after a repair is completed otherwise it may never come off.

Brighten up dull glassware temporarily by rubbing it over with olive oil and gently buffing it up with a soft cloth.

ORNAMENTS AND JEWELLERY

Removing polish deposits from intricate metalware

Wear an overall and cover your work surface with old newspaper. Ventilate the room as the fumes can be very unpleasant. Dip an old clean toothbrush into a container of household ammonia and carefully apply it to polish deposits in the crevices of ornate brass and copper trays and ornaments. The deposits will soften almost immediately and you will be able to brush them out.

Mending a foot on a copper kettle or plantholder

Copper can be soldered so you should be able to attach a missing foot or leg by this method. You will need resin-cored solder and a soldering iron or a soldering attachment for a blowlamp, eg the **Taymar LG870** blowlamp (available from DIY shops and hardware stores). Clean the area to be soldered with a file or by scraping with a small knife. You will probably need another person to hold the foot or leg in position with a pair of pliers while you use the iron or attachment.

Replacing broken box hinges

Broken hinges cannot be repaired and should be replaced. Small hinges are usually available from DIY shops or by mail order from W. Hobby Ltd, Knight's Hill Square, London SE27 0HH.

If the broken hinges are fixed with pins you will need to remove these carefully with pliers or a screwdriver, taking care not to damage the wood. Fit the new hinges using the old holes. If the holes are enlarged, fill them with pieces of matchstick or plastic wood.

Repairing chips in lacquer boxes

Fill the chips with **Fine Surface Polyfilla** and, when dry, rub them down gently with fine glasspaper. Finish to match the rest of the box with a paint such as **Humbrol Enamel** applied with a fine art brush.

Valuable lacquer boxes should be repaired by an expert.

Renewing a baize-covered base

If baize on the bases of vases or candlesticks has been damaged or come loose, it can cause scratching on highly polished surfaces so it is important to renew it.

Carefully scrape off the remains of the old baize with a knife. Use a little warm water to dissolve the original adhesive and be sure that it is all removed before you apply the new covering.

Use a self-adhesive material such as **Fablon Velour** which looks like baize and is easy to cut to size and fix. Just peel off the thin backing paper and apply the pre-cut material to the base. Buy it from hardware shops and Woolworth's in black, brown, red or green.

It is also possible to use small pieces of felt which can be bought in squares or by the metre in many colours. It is available from most department stores and craft shops. Glue them on with adhesive, eg **Copydex**.

Repairing costume jewellery

When glueing two different substances together (eg glass and metal) use an epoxy resin adhesive such as **Araldite Rapid**, taking care not to get it on any surface other than those to be stuck. Hold the repair in position with some adhesive tape (**Sellotape**) while it dries.

If the piece of jewellery is valuable or of sentimental value the repair should be done professionally by a jeweller.

Rethreading a string of beads

Use a nylon bead threader kit which is available from larger branches of Woolworth's. Before removing all the beads from the old string, check to see if the string is knotted and at what intervals. You must repeat this sequence in order to end up with the right length.

With beads of graduated size it will help if you spread them and grade them for size along the centre fold of a tall book open at the middle page—a child's colouring book is ideal as it is slim enough to open fairly flat. When you have graded them into order you will be able to see if any are missing.

Follow the threading instructions supplied with the kit and make the knots by looping the thread beyond the bead, passing the free thread through the loop and holding a thick sewing needle in the loop to draw it as close to the bead as possible while you tighten the string to form the knot. Remove the needle and continue threading and knotting in sequence.

Replacing a fastener on a brooch

Use either a safety pin or a gilt or silverplate bar pin and catch. These are available from arts and crafts shops. Glue either type of fastening to the back of the brooch with an epoxy resin adhesive such as **Bostik 7** or **Araldite Rapid**.

Glueing stones back on to costume jewellery

Use a clear adhesive, eg **Bostik 1 Clear**. If the piece contains semi-precious stones, seek professional advice from a jeweller.

Cleaning heavily tarnished brass and copper

Remove any lacquer on a brass or copper object or you will not be able to polish it to a good shine. Use paint stripper, **Knobs and Knockers Lacquer Remover** or **Joy Takes-it-off**, following the manufacturer's instructions. Wear gloves and work in a well-ventilated room.

Wash the item in a warm solution of washing-up liquid. Brush it gently with a soft brush (hard bristles could scratch), then rinse and dry with a soft cloth. Once all the general dirt is removed you will be able to see the extent of the tarnish.

Light tarnish can usually be removed with metal polish. Heavy tarnish first needs to be rubbed with a lemon cut in half, and the flesh dipped in salt. Although the lemon should work into most intricate mouldings, you may need to use a soft toothbrush to get into very tight corners. Take care not to leave the lemon and salt on the metal for too long or it will cause dark marks to form which need long hard polishing to remove. Once the tarnish has gone, rinse the item in warm water, then polish as usual.

Corroded copper and brass need stronger treatment from something like **Knobs and Knockers Corrosion Remover**.

Lacquering brass and copper

Once polished, you can maintain the shine on brass and copper for longer if you lacquer it. Do bear in mind that lacquer will slightly alter the colour of the metal and may make it look artificial. You will have to remove the lacquer from time to time in order to repolish the metal (see above).

Good lacquers are **Knobs and Knockers Clear Lacquer** and **Solvol Clear Protector** which is an aerosol and easier to apply to large items than lacquer on a brush.

Removing candlewax from candlesticks

Let the wax set, then chip off as much as possible with your finger-nails. Stand the candlestick upright on an old newspaper and play a hair dryer over the remaining deposit to melt the wax so that it will run off.

Wash the candlestick in warm soapy water where possible (taking care not to wet a baize-covered base), then clean and polish the candlestick according to the type of metal.

Remember . . .

Don't attempt to repair even cheap items of small and delicate jewellery unless you have the special tools required.

When cleaning metals such as silver, brass and copper, don't leave them in the cleaning solution too long as this may cause discoloration.

Metal that is to be soldered must be thoroughly clean otherwise the solder will not take. Use a file to clean the surface of the metal until new metal shows through.

When applying baize or self-adhesive material to the base of porous ornaments, you must first seal the surface. A coat of varnish applied and allowed to dry will overcome the porosity.

Self-adhesive tape used to hold a repair in position while the glue dries should be removed as soon as possible, otherwise it may be difficult to get off.

It's always well worthwhile getting valuable jewellery insured against loss or theft, but be sure to have the jewellery valued every year or so to check the insurance cover is adequate.

Valuable rings, especially those with raised or claw settings, should be cleaned regularly and it's a good idea to have the settings checked from time to time by a jeweller.

ELECTRICAL REPAIRS

Electrical safety

If in doubt about any electrical equipment or procedure, consult a qualified electrician.

Turn off mains switch and remove fuses before working on any electrical fitting.

Have your wiring checked every five years by a qualified electrician and have any wiring that's over 25 years old renewed.

Appliances Always unplug appliances that are not in use, particularly television and radio sets.

Switch off appliances before pulling their plugs from their sockets.

Switch off and disconnect any appliance before working on it.

Always follow the manufacturer's instructions when using any electrical appliance.

Never use any portable appliance in the bathroom, except an electric shaver, and then only from a special shaver socket (see drawing).

Never poke implements into electrical equipment like toasters or fires. If something gets lodged in a toaster, unplug it and turn it upside-down and shake it.

Never get into bed with an electric under-blanket switched on, unless

it's low voltage or a special type that is intended to be left on.

Plugs and socket outlets Always buy good quality plugs conforming to BS1363 and check them all frequently to make sure that the terminals and cover haven't worked loose, the flex is securely fixed in the flex grip and there are no bare wires poking through the sides. Replace a plug if it becomes broken or cracked.

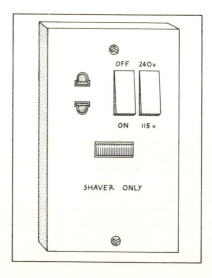

Fit smash-proof plugs to equipment that is moved around a lot, such as vacuum cleaners or electric drills.

Test outlets before touching them by plugging in an appliance you know is working.

Never poke anything into a socket outlet other than the plug intended to fit it. Modern sockets have shutters that close over when the plug is pulled out. For the older type of socket—especially in homes with small children—it's wise to fit some kind of shield.

Never put two-pin plugs into three-pin sockets.

Never overload socket outlets by using multi-plug adaptors. It is safer to install a double socket outlet (see page 70).

Flexes Never repair flex with adhesive or insulating tape. Replace old, frayed or damaged flex with new flex. Use a connector unit to extend a flex (see below).

Never tuck flexes under floor coverings or lay them where they could become damp or wet. Avoid trailing lengths of flex between plugs and appliances. They are easily tripped over and continually walking over a flex will damage its insulation and cause overheating and eventually fire.

Lighting Metal light fittings, whether ceiling-fixed or on standard or table lamps, must have the metal parts earthed. Never use them from a two-pin plug or on an unearthed socket outlet.

Never plug an appliance into a lamp holder or use a lighting circuit for anything more than the maximum wattage it is intended to carry.

Extending a flex

Never extend a flex by joining wires with insulating tape. For three-core flexes, use an enclosed flex connector (from Woolworth's and electrical dealers) with an earth terminal. Remove the plug from the appliance flex before you start.

Remove the plastic cover from the connector, taking care loose terminals do not drop out. Trim back the outer cover of the flex to expose the inner wires. Push the flex into the rubber sleeve in the connector, then through the cord grip, and pull it through far enough to connect it to the terminals. Trim away the insulation of the core wires if necessary.

Twist the strands of each wire neatly, then connect each wire to the correct terminal in the flex connector. Be sure to connect the green and yellow earth wire to the earth terminal. Tighten up cord grip screws

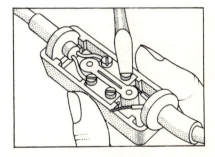

and replace the cover on the connector.

While a flex connector is the best solution for extending flexes on lamps, sewing machines and domestic appliances, it is better to use an extension lead on power tools and other portable appliances such as vacuum cleaners. Before using an extension lead, make sure it is fully uncoiled or unwound from its reel otherwise it may heat up.

Wiring a 13-amp plug

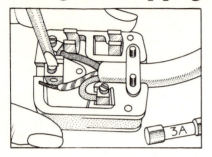

The wires in a flex are colour coded:

Brown	= LIVE
Blue	= NEUTRAL
Green and yellow	= EARTH

The terminals in the plug to which each should be connected are labelled L, N and E.

With a screwdriver, undo the centre screw of the plug and take off the cover. Loosen the two small screws that hold the cord grip in place and remove one of them. Push the cord grip to one side. Remove the cartridge fuse and loosen the screws in the terminals but do not remove them or allow them to fall out.

Trim the outer sleeve of the flex back about 5 cm. Strip the coloured insulation from the three core wires back about 1 cm. Twist the bare wires neatly. Put the flex into the plug, replace the screw in the cord grip and tighten the grip into position, making sure it sits over the outer insulation of the flex, not the inner wires. Fix the wires to the correct terminals and tighten the screws to trap the bare wire. Make sure there are no loose strands of wire.

Replace the cartridge fuse. Fit a 3-amp fuse for appliances rated at 720 W or less, and a 13-amp fuse for those between 720 W and 3000 W. Replace the cover of the plug and tighten the central screw.

Some appliances, known as double-insulated appliances, are fitted with two-wire flexes which have no green and yellow (earth) wire. When fitting a plug to such an appliance, leave the earth terminal blank and fit the two wires to the appropriate terminals.

Replacing flex on an iron (or similar appliance)

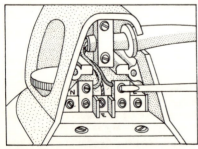

Disconnect the appliance by removing the plug from the socket before you start. On the appliance, take out the screws holding the terminal cover or back panel over the flex entry and lift off the cover. Undo the terminal screws, noting carefully where each wire goes (draw a diagram if you think you'll forget). If it looks too complicated, don't attempt the job yourself; take the appliance to your local electrical repair shop. If the wires have sleeves of flexible heat-resistant tubing over them, remove these and retain them for use on the new flex.

Take the old flex with you when you go to buy a replacement as it is vital to get one of the correct rating for the appliance.

Strip back the outer cover on the

new flex by about 5 cm and expose each core wire by about 1.5 cm. Twist the bare wires neatly, then refit any heat-resistant sleeves. Connect the new flex carefully to the correct terminals and tighten them up firmly. Replace the terminal cover.

For appliances with a separate flex, such as an electric kettle, the task is simpler. Remove the connector and plug from the old appliance flex. Buy a correctly rated new flex and attach the connector and plug to it. On some appliances, such as electric fires and fans, you may need to remove a panel to get to the terminal block.

Repairing a blown fuse

Ring circuit wiring A modern ring circuit has two types of fuse as a protection against overloading—a small cartridge fuse in each plug and a main fuse in the consumer unit or fuse box. In houses with modern wiring, if an appliance stops working, switch off at once, both at the appliance itself and at the socket outlet. Remove the plug, unscrew the cover, take out the cartridge fuse and click in a new one. Be sure to use a fuse with the correct rating (3- or 13-amp) for the job. Do not rely on the blown fuse as a guide as it may have been wrong in the first place.

On most appliances you will find the wattage rating plate either on the base or on the back. Use a 3-amp fuse for anything up to 720 watts, such as lamps and electric blankets, and a 13-amp fuse for appliances with a loading of between 720 and 3000 watts, such as a kettle, iron, radiant heater or washing machine. Using too small a fuse will cause it to blow. Refrigerators, freezers and vacuum cleaners usually have a 13-amp fuse fitted, even though the loading is below 720 watts, because their motors need a high starting current. A colour television needs a 13-amp fuse.

Radial circuit wiring If you live in old property or if you still have the old type of radial circuit wiring, your plugs may be the round-pin, unfused type and you will probably have an old-type fuse box and switch. In this case, if trouble occurs, eg if an appliance stops working, you will have to trace the fault back to the fuse box. Switch off the appliance and remove the plug from the socket. Find the main switch controlling the circuit and switch this off. Trace the blown fuse in the fuse box by removing one fuse at a time. The blown one will be immediately noticeable by the melted fuse wire and blackened fuse holder. Make the job of finding a blown fuse easier by labelling each fuse in the box beforehand so that it is easy to tell which fuse belongs to which circuit and which rooms or appliances it serves. Do this either by a process of elimination (ie by removing each fuse in turn and going round the house testing to see which appliances or lights don't come on) or by calling in an electrician to sort it out for you. Replace the blown fuse with fuse wire of the correct size.

Always have in your tool kit at least one spare cartridge fuse of all sizes or a card with the different sizes of fuse wire used in your fuse box.

Main fuse If a main fuse blows, first turn off the mains switch. This may be on the consumer unit or on a separate switch box nearby. There are three types of main fuse you may find in your fuse box. A modern fuse box will have cartridge fuses. A *cartridge fuse* is an insulated cylinder with a cap at each end like a plug cartridge, but with a different current rating and bigger diameter. These you replace in the same way as plug fuses (see page 67). An older-type fuse box may have protected fuses or bridge fuses. In a *protected fuse*, the wire is threaded through a protective porcelain cover. You will need to remove this cover by loosening the screw at the end to see if the wire is burnt. If so, thread through a new piece of wire of the correct current rating. Do not strain the wire too much when tightening the terminals. In a *bridge fuse*, the wire is held at either end of a small hump, or bridge. If the fuse has blown, you will be able to see that the wire has broken or melted. Replace as for a protected fuse.

Fitting a new ceiling lampholder

Buy a new plastic lampholder (the accessory which holds the electric light bulb) from an electrical shop. Switch off at the mains and remove the fuse from the consumer unit or fuse box (see page 67). Check that the light does not work.

Remove the lampshade and bulb, if necessary, and take off the old holder. Trim the insulation of the hanging flex with wire cutters. Twist the wires of each lead into single strands and pinch over at the end for easier threading.

Unscrew the top of the new holder and thread the flex through it. Position the leads each side of the anchorage on the holder. Connect a wire to each terminal and tighten the screws. Screw the holder together and fit the light bulb and lampshade. Replace the fuse, switch on at the mains and test that the light works.

Replacing a light switch with a dimmer switch

Do not do this yourself if you have old wiring in your home and the protruding type of light switch. Instead, get a professional electrician to do the job for you.

With modern wiring, first switch off at the mains and remove the fuse from the consumer unit or fuse box (see page 67). Check that the light does not switch on. Undo the screws which hold the existing switch in the wall box. Pull the switch forward carefully and undo the red and black wires from the terminals on the switch. Do not remove the green earth wire which is normally connected to a third terminal fixed on to the wall box.

Following the instructions supplied with the dimmer switch, connect up the red and black wires to the appropriate terminals. Place the dimmer switch in the wall box and fix it in place with the two screws.

Replace the fuse in the consumer unit and turn on the mains switch. Check the dimmer is working properly.

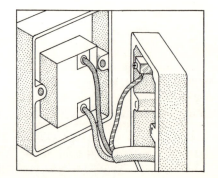

Replacing an electric fire element

Unplug the fire from the socket outlet. If it is a fixed appliance, switch off at the mains and remove the fuse from the consumer unit (see page 67). Take off the safety guard which will be held by clips or screws.

To expose the element connectors on an infra-red sheathed element, you must remove the end covers. These will either slide off or be held in position by two screws. Unscrew the milled terminal nuts, using a pair of grips or pliers if they are tight. Take care not to apply too much pressure or the brackets may distort.

Gently apply sideways pressure to the element so that it springs away from the terminal brackets. Carefully lift the element forwards and remove it from the fire.

If the terminals are corroded, clean them with fine abrasive paper. Take the opportunity to clean up the reflector while the element is out. Wipe it over with a cloth wrung out in a solution of washing-up liquid (never use an abrasive). Dry the surface and buff up well with a soft duster. Buy a new element of the correct type from an electrical dealer.

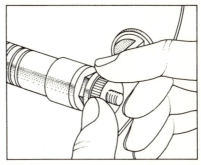

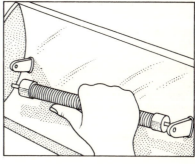

Take the old one with you to check it against the replacement. Fit the new element, replace the guard and test the fire.

Replacing the starter on a fluorescent light fitting

If the tube lights up but goes out after a few seconds, or just flickers and will not light up, it is most likely to be the starter that is broken. The starter is an automatic switch that operates the tube circuit. It cannot be repaired so the old one must be removed and replaced with a new one from an electrical shop.

Before carrying out any repairs to the light, switch off the electricity at the mains and remove the fuse from the fuse box.

The starter is situated either inside the casing of the light fitting or projecting from the side—it is a small canister about 2 cm in diameter and 4 cm long. To remove the starter, turn it anti-clockwise. Take it with you when you go to buy the new one to be sure of buying the correct type.

Fit the new starter into the light fitting by turning it clockwise. Replace the fuse and switch on the mains before testing the light.

Changing a single socket outlet to a double

First, switch off the electricity at the mains and remove the fuse from the fuse box (see page 67). It's very important to double-check that the electricity is off by plugging in a table lamp as a test.

Unscrew the screws holding the socket into the metal wall box. Carefully pull the socket forwards and unscrew the terminal screws.

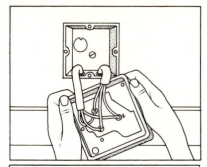

Remove the cables from the terminals and take off the socket outlet. If the cables are too short to fit a double socket, call an electrician.

Unscrew the metal box and remove it from the wall. Hold the new box up and mark the outline of it on the wall. Cut away the plaster and brickwork within the outline with a hammer and cold chisel, taking care not to damage the cables.

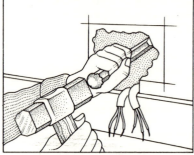

Drill new fixing holes in the brickwork, using a masonry bit, and plug the holes. Knock out the metal entry discs in the box and push the cables through. Fix the box into position.

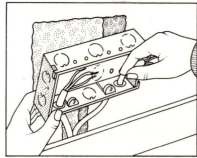

Re-plaster around the edges of the box and the section of wall carrying the cables. Smooth off the plaster with a trowel or filling knife and leave to dry overnight.

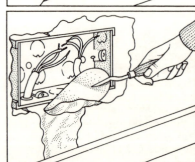

Connect the two lots of cables to the new double socket outlet. The red wires should be attached to the LIVE terminals, the black to the NEUTRAL and the green to the EARTH. Fit the new socket outlet into the metal wall box and replace the screws. Replace the fuse in the fuse box, switch on at the mains and test the outlet.

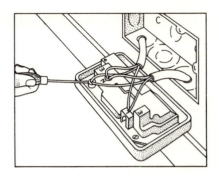

Replacing the element on a non-automatic kettle

Remove the flex and plug. Stand the kettle on a firm work surface and unscrew the coupling (ie where you plug into the appliance). If it is too tight to unscrew by hand, use pipe grips and protect the coupling from damage by wrapping a cloth round it. Take off the remains of the old fibre washers and throw them away. New washers will be supplied with the new element. Use a twisting action to release the element from the kettle body.

Carefully slide the element inwards and away from the kettle body. Lift it out through the lid opening at the top of the kettle. Take the old element or the complete kettle with you to buy a replacement element from your local electrical dealer.

Clean out both sides of the element hole in the kettle body, using a knife to scrape off any build-up of scale. Take care not to distort the sides of the hole. Fit the new washer to the threaded section of the element. Then carefully follow the manufacturer's instructions for the sequence of fitting actions.

Replace the element in the kettle, checking first that it is the correct way up (this should be stamped on the casing). Fit the outer washer and screw on the coupling. Fill the kettle with water and test.

Fitting a new element into an automatic kettle is much more complicated and should be done by a professional electrician. Many small electrical shops offer this service.

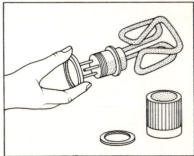

Cleaning an electric shaver

Before doing any maintenance, unplug from the mains and remove the lead.

You should follow manufacturers' instructions for all cleaning and maintenance.

Generally speaking, an electric shaver should be cleaned after every use with the brush provided, taking care not to damage delicate sections, such as the cutters and covers.

Every so often, give the shaver a complete clean, if recommended by the manufacturer, using their cleaning fluid. This may involve dismantling the heads or cutters and you should follow directions closely when doing this.

For replacements or repairs, take the shaver to the appropriate service agent.

Replacing a drive belt on an upright vacuum cleaner

The drive belt needs replacing when the vacuum cleaner's motor works but the brush roller does not rotate. Check details of the model number on the vacuum cleaner name plate before you go to buy the new belt. The wrong belt will not fit.

The drive belt is situated either at the front of the cleaner or underneath. Remove the cover which is usually held in place by spring clips or a metal catch. Lift out the roller and remove the worn or broken drive belt. Slide the new belt over the roller and fit it back into the cleaner. Stretch the belt until it fits over the drive pulley. Check with the instruction book that it is on the right way round or it will spring off as soon as you switch the cleaner on again.

Remember . . .

If you make a mistake in woodwork, plumbing or decorating, it can be put right at a little extra cost. If you make a mistake with electrical work, you may not get a second chance. Faulty work could prove lethal to you or to somebody else. If you are not confident about what you plan to do, do not attempt it—call a qualified electrician. *Be sure to read the electrical safety rules on page 64 before carrying out any electrical repair.*

Always bear in mind the colour coding for flexes before re-wiring a plug, or doing some other repair. The colour coding for flexes (see page 66) is different from that for main supply wiring (see page 71).

Check the condition of your electrical appliances regularly and carry out any necessary repairs. Never use an old appliance about which you are doubtful without having it checked by an electrician.

Keep your electrical tools (see page 118) where they can always be found, even in the dark! Keep them in a special box, separate from your other DIY tools.

Any electrical lighting installed outside the house must be weather-proofed and is best controlled from switches inside the house.

Wiring for outdoor electrical installations must always be done by a qualified electrician.

PIPES, TANKS AND RADIATORS

Releasing a jammed stopcock

The stopcock is like a tap except it is connected into the main water supply pipework. It acts as a valve which can be closed when necessary to stop the water supply, such as in an emergency to prevent flooding, or when it is necessary to drain down the pipes in order to work on the plumbing. You will find stopcocks at various points in the plumbing system, eg where the water supply comes into the house, or at the point where the water supply leaves the storage cistern, etc. This is so the system can be isolated and/or drained when necessary.

Stopcocks often become jammed if they are not used. To release one that is stiff, apply some aerosol lubricant, such as **Rocket WD40** (available from hardware and car accessory shops), leave it for a few minutes and then carefully rotate the stopcock. If it is completely seized up you will need to call a plumber.

Eliminating airlocks in the water supply

Airlocks in the water supply result in the water coming out of the tap in trickles or spurts and finally stopping. This is usually accompanied by knocking noises in the pipes. You can correct this yourself if you have separate hot and cold mains taps, usually in the kitchen, but if you have a mixer tap you will need to call a plumber.

To cure the problem, you will need a short length of hosepipe, two adjustable hose clips and a screwdriver. Use the clips to fit the hose in a U-shape between the hot and cold (mains) taps. Tighten the clips with a screwdriver so they are a good fit. Turn on washbasin and bath taps to allow air to escape.

Turn on first the hot and then the cold water tap and let them run together for a few minutes. The theory is that the mains pressure through the cold tap will force water and air back through the pipes up into the hot water storage tank or cylinder and so clear the airlock. If it does not work the first time, try again. If you have no success after about 20 minutes call a plumber.

74

Repairing a leak in a copper water pipe

If a pipe leaks at the point where it is connected to a fitting, it may be that one of the nuts on the end of the compression fitting has worked loose. Carefully tighten up the nut with a spanner. If the pipe itself is damaged, you can repair the hole temporarily with a resin product such as **David's Isopon**. Bind over the damaged area with an old bandage or strip of fabric.

A permanent repair can be made with **Beat-a-Burst** repair clamps which come in various sizes to fit all domestic pipes. Buy them at DIY shops or from DMC Products,

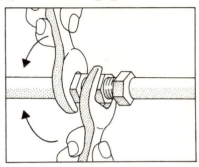

Victoria Mill, Wilton Street, Denton, Manchester M34 3HB.

Stopping an overflow from a storage cistern

The storage cistern supplies water to the washbasins, baths, sinks, etc., in the house. As in the loo cistern, flow into the storage cistern is controlled by a ball valve fixed to an arm and ball float. An overflow may be caused by the ball float being damaged, the float arm being too high or the valve being faulty. If the ball float is damaged, unscrew it and replace it with a new plastic one (from DIY or hardware shops). While waiting to repair it, you can effect an emergency repair by tying a plastic bag round the ball after first emptying it of any water which may have got inside. If the overflow is being caused by the float arm being too high, or a faulty valve, see page 38.

Improving pipe lagging

Wrap pipes with strips of glass fibre, allowing an overlap of about half the width of the strip as you wind it round. Tie into position with string or tape. When joining lengths, overlap well so there are no gaps.

Where there are taps it is a good idea to wrap the stems separately and bandage the glass fibre strip on to the pipe. Leave tap heads and valves uncovered for easy access.

An alternative method of lagging pipes is to use pre-formed foam plastic which you buy in 1-m lengths. Dunlop make this in a variety of diameters to fit different-sized pipes. Buy it from DIY and hardware shops and builders' merchants. You just slip the cover over the pipe and fix it with adhesive tape.

Curing noisy water pipes (water hammer)

Knocking in the pipes when mains water taps are turned on is often caused by loose pipework or a damaged ball float in the storage cistern. Check the ball float (see page 75) and replace it, if necessary, and call a plumber to make the pipework secure with extra pipe clips.

Water hammer can also be caused by deterioration of the gland packing or a loose gland nut in the mains water tap. To tighten up the gland nut, remove the crosstop and chrome cover of the tap by unscrewing the grub screw. Carefully tighten the gland nut with an adjustable spanner

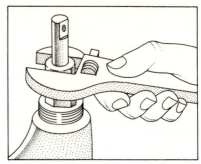

and replace the cover and crosstop. If this does not cure the problem, it will probably be necessary to call a plumber to fit a new tap.

Thawing frozen pipes

If water left in the U trap under a sink or basin is frozen, wrap cloths wrung out in very hot water round the trap. Wear rubber gloves to protect your hands from scalding. Do not pour hot water into a porcelain sink or basin which has frozen up as the sudden temperature change could crack it.

Other frozen pipes can be thawed out in the same way, or by applying warm air from a hair dryer. Never use a blowlamp to do this as the risk of fire is too great. Work the hair dryer along the frozen section of the pipe, starting from the tap and working towards the tank. Take very great care in confined spaces, such as lofts and cupboards, as you could ignite dust and cause a fire.

Thawing out a frozen cistern valve

Pour boiling water from a kettle over the ball valve. Gently work the arm up and down until it is free. Do not exert too much pressure or it will break.

Removing rust from pipes

Rust occurs because bare ferrous metal (iron and steel) becomes exposed to the air. If allowed to persist, rust will eventually destroy the metal.

Wear goggles to protect your eyes and gloves to protect your hands when dealing with rust. Use a scraper or wire brush to remove as much as possible. Really severe rusting may need to be removed with a wire brush attachment on a power drill.

When all the rust is removed and you can see only clean metal, wipe or brush off all the loose dust. Apply a good even coat of metal primer and when dry apply undercoat and top-coat.

For small areas of rust, it is sometimes easier to use a chemical rust remover such as **Kurust** (which would be expensive used over large areas). Rub off any loose rust, grease and dust and apply the remover with a brush. Wash it off with water or spirit according to the manufacturer's instructions. When dry, apply undercoat and topcoat. After using most chemical rust removers it is unnecessary to prime the metal before painting.

Hiding pipes where paint is peeling off

Paint tends to peel off hot water pipes and the best solution is to insulate them with plastic sleeving, such as **Dunlop** pre-formed foam pipe insulation, and box them in with plywood. The box can be decorated with paper or paint to match the existing decor.

Remember . . .

If you put a shelf over a radiator it will prevent the wall above becoming soiled.

Corrosion can occur in the radiators of a central heating system, causing them to leak. To prevent damage, have the system flushed through and a corrosion inhibitor put into the header tank.

To help prevent the build-up of scale in a domestic hot water system, put an **Albright & Wilson Micromet** in your cold water storage cistern.

When insulating your water pipes and loft, do not neglect any taps and pipes in the garage, which also need insulation.

If you're going to be away from home for a short while during the winter, set your central heating to come on at a very low temperature for a few hours each day. If you are going away for a long time, it's best to drain the system down to avoid the risk of burst pipes.

There's no need to use a special paint on radiators—emulsion or gloss will do.

There are certain rules about the best positioning of central heating radiators in rooms to take into account when planning installation, so consult an expert.

OUTDOOR REPAIRS

Unblocking an outside drain

Remove the grille over the drain and scrub it well with a hot disinfectant solution such as **Jeyes Ibcol**. Wear household gloves to protect your hands.

Tie or tape an old spoon or trowel to a length of cane and use it to break up the blockage and lift the silt from the gully base. Scrape off any sludge which has collected on the inner walls of the drain with a trowel. Flush out with a bucket of clean water and brush the gully with a stiff bristle drain brush such as the **Kleeneze** which has an adjustable head so that you can get the right angle. Pour more disinfectant solution down the drain and replace the grille.

To prevent drains becoming blocked, do not put anything down them which cannot be flushed away. The worst culprits are large quantities of tea leaves or coffee grounds, vegetable peelings and grease. To prevent a build-up of grease, make it a weekly task to dissolve a cupful of washing soda crystals in a jug of very hot water and pour the solution down the drain.

Repairing damaged brickwork

Cracks in brickwork can be repaired easily. Remove loose debris and scrape the area clean with a cold chisel. Clear away dust with a wire brush and wet the brickwork thoroughly. Apply a building mastic such as **Homeseal Outdoor Sealant** with a standard squeeze gun (from DIY shops) and smooth it over with a trowel. This mastic comes in various colours to match existing brickwork.

Alternatively, use a standard mortar mix.

When several bricks are damaged, cut them away with a hammer and cold chisel until you reach sound brickwork. Take care not to bash too hard or you may loosen good brickwork. Clean the area, then fix new bricks in place with a mortar mix such as **Marleymix** bricklaying mortar and rendering mix.

Filling gaps between window frames and brickwork

Stop draughts coming in by filling these gaps with a mastic such as **Homeseal Outdoor Sealant** which comes in white, natural, grey and mahogany. Using the special applicator, squirt the mastic into the gap and level it off to give a good finish. These mastics remain flexible and can be sanded and painted if necessary.

Clearing out gutters

Gutters that are left to become blocked with leaves and debris cause rainwater to overflow and make walls damp.

Check that your ladder is stable and resting against the wall of the house and not the gutter itself. If your gutters are difficult to reach safely, get them cleared by a builder. Plug the opening of the downpipe with old rags or a wad of newspaper so that none of the debris blocks the downpipe and drain below, and clear out all loose debris with an old paintbrush. With a wire brush, go along the inside of the gutter to remove any rust if your guttering is metal. Apply a coat of bitumastic paint such as **Presomet** (from builders' merchants and hardware shops). Remove the plug from the downpipe opening and use a watering can to pour water down to check that it is clear.

Repairing gutters

Each year, check your gutters for leaks and fill faulty joints with putty or waterproof mastic. Tighten up any of the loose bolts which hold sections of the gutter together and replace badly worn ones with new. Refit new brackets where any are loose or broken or the gutters will start to sag. Take care when putting in new ones to maintain the slope towards the downpipe.

A clogged downpipe can often be cleared with a piece of wire or flexible cane. Pour a jug of hot water down afterwards to clear any debris. Protect the pipe from further clogging by covering the top with a plastic pipe grid or a piece of rigid plastic netting.

Eliminating damp patches on walls

These may be caused by a number of things such as damaged gutters (see above), or mortar (pointing) between the brickwork in need of replacement (see page 79), or subsidence causing walls to crack. If it is cracked walls that are causing the problem, you will need to get a builder to inspect them and advise you.

Provided the dampness has not penetrated the structure of the house, you can treat the outside of the walls with a damp-proofing solution such as **Cuprinol No More Damp Exterior Walls** which will repel rainwater. Just brush it on to the brick, stone or concrete surface and leave it to dry to a colourless finish that doesn't alter the appearance of the walls.

Dealing with rising damp

Your house may not have a damp-proof course or the damp-proof course may have become defective. If you suspect this may be the problem, get a surveyor to check it for you. Start by checking the outside brickwork at ground level. Any soil or rubbish that has piled up against it may be encouraging damp to cross the damp-proof course and creep up the wall. Rake away anything you find lying against the walls and brush off loose debris from the brickwork with a wire brush. Wear goggles to protect your eyes.

Paint the bottom 30 cm or so of the walls with a waterproofer such as **Synthaprufe** or **Cuprinol No More Damp Roofs/Walls**. Wait until the waterproofer is dry before replacing any soil and make sure that it does not go over the damp-proof course.

Replacing a dislodged roof tile

This is not a job for the amateur. A dislodged and crooked tile means that the nails holding it in place or the nibs (the projections on the underneath of the tile) have broken. Call in an expert at once—repair is cheaper than replacement of the entire roof. An expert will also be able to tell you if it is worthwhile repairing your roof in bits and pieces or whether it will be cheaper in the long run to have it re-roofed.

Details of roofing contractors are available from Redland Re-Roofing Advice Centre (see page 120).

Building up a worn step

Frequently used steps such as those outside back doors can become worn down in the centre and therefore dangerous. Build them up with an all-purpose filler such as **Tetrion**.

Clean the step thoroughly with a wire brush. Wear goggles to prevent particles getting in your eyes. Ensure that dust and any loose material is removed—a damp cloth is good for this—and that the step is completely dry. Apply the filler with a trowel and smooth it off neatly. A deep hollow will need several applications to give a good strong result. Put about 5 mm of filler on each time and allow it to dry before applying the next layer.

Stopping birds nesting in eaves

You can discourage nest-building in eaves by spraying along the top of the house walls and under the eaves with **Synchemicals' Stay-Off** available in 100-g sachets from most garden centres and shops. Synchemicals Ltd, 44 Grange Walk, London SE1 3EN will send a stockist list on receipt of a stamped addressed envelope.

Stay-Off makes up into a solution and is easiest to apply with the type of pressurised sprayer used for roses or fruit trees. It is also helpful for protecting seeds, bulbs, fruits and buds from the ravages of birds.

Preventing birds damaging thatch

Tackle this problem before the birds start building their nests but bear in mind that the solution is tricky and needs to be carried out by an expert. The thatch needs to be wired with galvanised 5-mm mesh (20 or 22 gauge). Advice on obtaining professional help is available from The Thatching Advisory Service (see page 120).

Removing old paint splashes from stone doorsteps

The quickest method is to use a blowlamp. Take care not to overheat the stone and keep the blowlamp moving continuously. Use a paint scraper at an almost horizontal angle to the step so that you scrape off the paint without scoring the stone.

If you don't have a blowlamp, scrub the step with an abrasive such as a wire brush or wire wool.

Cleaning and painting a wrought-iron gate

Remove the gate from its hinges and tighten them if necessary. Lubricate with oil before replacing the gate.

Remove old paint and rust with a wire brush taking care to wear goggles so that particles do not fly into your eyes. If rusting is extensive, use a chemical rust remover or a blowlamp. Apply a metal primer and then paint with an aerosol such as **Holts Handy Spray Gloss Paint**.

Repairing a wooden gate

Loose joints on a wooden gate cause strain on the hinges and can prevent it opening and closing properly. Remove the gate from its post and carefully prise the loose joints apart. Apply a wood glue such as **Evo-Stik Woodworking Adhesive** and hammer the joints back into position. Make a string tourniquet (see page 51) to hold them in position while the adhesive dries. Wipe off surplus adhesive before it has time to set.

Broken joints or weak sections should be strengthened by fixing a steel angle or T bracket to both sides of the damaged piece. Apply metal primer to the brackets as soon as possible to prevent them rusting. You can cover with metal paint.

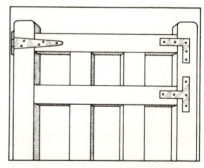

If the gate is sagging, you will need to adjust the hinges. Refix them by plugging the old holes with wood plugs and putting in new screws. Use a little grease on the screw threads to make them easier to insert.

Repairing cracks or holes in a garden path

Remove all loose debris from any holes. Using a chisel, go round the edges, cutting them back to sound concrete to a depth of about 3.5 cm. Remove all dust from the hole, either with a damp rag or with an outdoor vacuum cleaner.

If you are repairing a small area, buy ready-mixed sand and cement, eg **Marleymix Ready-Bagged Dry Mixes**. Otherwise, mix three parts sand to one part cement and make up with water and **Unibond Universal Adhesive** using the quantities recommended by the manufacturer. Wet the hole thoroughly and fill with the new concrete, pressing down firmly with a piece of wood. Smooth off the top with a trowel or smooth piece of wood so that the new filler lies level with the surrounding surface.

Cracks can be repaired in the same way but, when chiselling out the damaged parts, slope the sides inwards so that the concrete can spread out and grip the sides of the crack.

Paths or steps which have sunk slightly can be built up and levelled off with a thin layer of concrete. First

clean the area to be treated, then prime the surface with a solution of PVA adhesive, eg **Unibond Universal**. Apply the concrete with a trowel and level off.

Replacing a broken gate post

You will need to buy a new post from a timber merchant or garden centre. Dig out the old post and remove enough earth to enable you to set the new post at least 40–45 cm into the ground. Fill around the base with broken bricks and stones, and concrete over them. Use a spirit level to check that the post is upright and not set in at an angle.

Repairing a plastic plant container

If the container is cracked, stick it together with an epoxy resin such as **Araldite**. A broken section can be remoulded with special putty such as **Tuf-Stuf Epoxy Repair Putty** which will bond to the original material. When dry, file or sand into a conforming shape.

Mending a garden fence

Repair broken fences before they
reach a stage when they have to be
replaced. Rotten posts can be
strengthened with a wooden or
concrete support at the base. First
treat the old wood with preservative,
then dig a 60 cm deep hole at the
base of the old support for the prop.
This will allow for the new support to
project about 60 cm up the old post.
Support the main post and fence with
struts while you are digging.

Push the prop into the hole and
ram broken bricks around the base to
hold it. Fill up the hole with concrete
and fix the support to the post, using
bolts supplied with the new support.

Repair broken arris rails (the
horizontal supports) with special
metal brackets available from
builders' merchants. Fix each bracket
with galvanised screws, taking care
to support the rail from the other side
while exerting pressure on it.

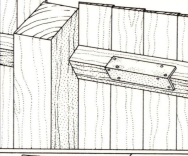

Rails that are beyond repair should
be replaced. First remove the fencing
boards then saw out the arris rails as
these are usually rebated into the
post. Refix new arris rails with arris
rail brackets or metal angle brackets
(available from timber merchants and
garden centres), using good
galvanised screws.

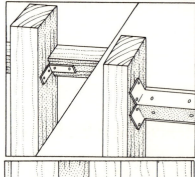

Replace a rotting gravel board to
protect the base of the fence from
rising damp. Dig earth away from the
fence and remove the old board.
Replace with a new board fixed to
wooden battens on the base of the
upright posts.

Treat all new wood with
preservative before fixing in place
and, when doing repairs, give the
whole fence a good coating of wood
preservative such as **Cuprinol Wood
Preserver**.

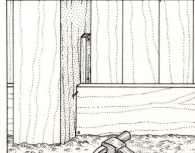

Replacing roofing felt

Buy roofing felt by the roll from hardware shops and builders' merchants. Fix it in overlapping layers with galvanised nails or an adhesive such as **Bostik 2 Weatherproof Adhesive**.

Where roofing felt is in poor condition but not yet in need of replacement, renovate it with a special waterproof sealant such as **Cover Plus Waterproof Roofing** which is available in several colours.

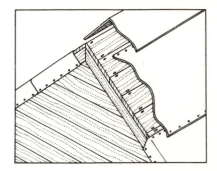

Cleaning a glass roof

Apart from general dirt, algae and moss tend to collect between overlapping panes on greenhouse or conservatory roofs. Use a hose in conjunction with a long-bristled brush to clean the glass and get between the panes where possible. Then, with the same brush, apply a solution of a bactericide, such as **Fungo**. Two applications may be required. Wear old clothes and goggles for protection.

Stopping a corrugated iron roof leaking

Wait for a dry day. Using a wire brush, remove loose dust and rust from the areas where the sheets overlap. Wear goggles and gloves to protect yourself. Cover the seams with **Sylglas Roof Repair Tape**. If you have to get on to the roof to do the repair, lay a board across it to spread your weight and make working easier.

Repairing a punctured airbed

Patching a slashed or punctured airbed isn't always satisfactory. Use the repair fluid **PVX** which comes in a small plastic bottle with an applicator nozzle. Slightly inflate the bed to prevent the top and bottom sticking together and apply the fluid over the slit. Leave to dry for about two hours. A large slit in the airbed may need two applications.

Removing a bird's nest from a chimney

This should be dealt with as soon as you discover it. A blocked chimney can be dangerous, causing fumes to blow back into the room which could be fatal. Turn off the boiler or put out the fire immediately.

Get a chimney sweep to clear the chimney (see page 12).

Curing a leaking pond

A cement-lined pond can develop hairline cracks due to temperature change, badly mixed cement or earth movement. To safeguard your pond against the effects of freezing in winter, float some pieces of polystyrene in the pond to counteract the expansion of the water as it turns to ice.

To repair a leaking pond, first drain it completely by bailing out as much water as possible and then allowing the remainder to drain through the cracks. Scrape out the cracks with a cold chisel and fill with **Blue Hawk Quick Setting Cement**. Alternatively, if there are lots of cracks, coat the whole surface with a PVA adhesive such as **Unibond Universal** following the manufacturer's instructions. When the adhesive is dry, apply a very thin layer of concrete over it.

Renewing split deckchair canvas

A small split in deckchair canvas can be repaired with a canvas or hessian patch cut larger than the damaged area. Stick the patch on with **Copydex Adhesive**.

Rotting canvas needs to be replaced with new fabric. Deckchair canvas is available off the roll from department stores, and chair covers made to size are also available from garden centres.

On a wooden-framed chair, fix the canvas with staples using a staple gun like the **Swingline Staple Gun**. These can be hired but are useful for all sorts of DIY jobs so it's probably worth investing in one. On tubular metal chairs, sew the canvas round the frame using thick thread and an upholstery or darning needle.

Mending a hosepipe

To repair a small leaking section, bind it with plastic, self-adhesive tape. **Copydex Pipe and Hose Seal** is available from DIY shops and gardening centres. Alternatively, a small damaged section can be cut out and the pipe rejoined with **Hozelock Connectors**. These are also useful for extending a hosepipe by joining two lengths together. They can be bought from hardware shops and garden centres.

If the plastic has deteriorated in several places, repair will not repay the effort. You will need to buy a new hosepipe.

Remember . . .

Do not carry out work with concrete in frosty weather as this will cause it to crack and disintegrate and your repair will be a weak one.

In very hot weather, cover a fresh concrete repair with wet sacks or paper to prevent it drying out too quickly.

Cover steps and patio areas before doing any house-painting jobs. Paint splashes are very difficult to remove from concrete and stone.

Before replacing a garden fence, check with your neighbour and local authority to ensure that the fence or wall you plan to put up will not contravene any local authority regulations or legal covenants.

Garden tools are expensive, so take care of them. Always clean them after use and put them away in a dry place.

It's better, and more economical in the long run, to buy rust-resistant garden tools, but if yours aren't, lightly spray the metal parts with **Rocket WD40** before storing them.

SECURITY

Making louvre windows secure

With some louvre windows it is possible for a burglar to remove the panes of glass from the outside by just lifting them out. To avoid this you can glue each end of the glass into the end of each louvre with an epoxy resin adhesive such as **Araldite**. This will fix the glass so it cannot be lifted out.

A somewhat unsightly alternative (but the best for security purposes) which allows you to open and close the window is to fit wooden battens across the opening, or a metal grill over the inside. These are available from specialist shops such as Banham's (see page 120).

Making old windows secure

It is possible to make most types of old window secure. There are various locks and attachments, such as those made by **Chubb** and **Copydex**, to suit casement and sash windows in wood and metal. For example, **Copydex** have window stay locks, lockable latches and special latch locks for metal windows that can be fitted without having to drill into the metal. Buy these from DIY shops, Woolworth's and department stores.

Making drainpipes burglarproof

Drainpipes make handy climbing poles for determined burglars. Paint them with **Anticlimb Paint** which doesn't dry and stays slippery. **Anticlimb** is available in six colours from hardware shops or from the manufacturers, Camrex Special Coating Services Ltd, Camrex House, PO Box 34, Sunderland. Check the cost of paint and carriage before ordering—and be sure you don't get marked with it!

Fitting a mortice lock

Mark a line in the centre of the door edge where you want to position the lock. Hold the lock against the door stile (see page 22) and with a sharp pencil mark the outline of the lock casing on to the door edge.

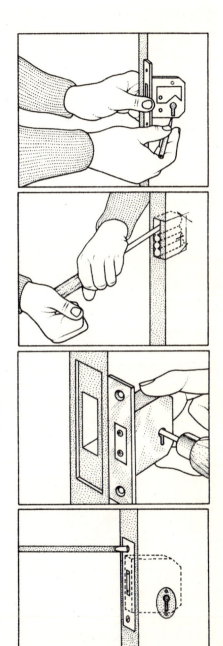

Drill a vertical row of holes the same diameter as the lock width and the depth of the casing. Drill the holes as close together as possible and then clean out the waste with a wood chisel. Test fit the lock and adjust the size of the cavity if necessary.

Chisel out a shallow recess for the face plate so that the lock will be flush with the door edge. Hold the lock against the face of the door and mark the position of the keyhole. Drill a hole to the right diameter and finish it off with a chisel or small padsaw. Make the keyhole slightly larger than the key.

Fit the escutcheon plates. Mark the position of the face plate screws. Fit the new lock and test the key in the keyhole. Screw the face plate to the door edge.

Close the door and turn the key. Mark the position of the striker plate on the door jamb and chisel out a recess to fit it. Screw the striker plate into position. Test the lock.

Fitting locks to external doors

All external doors should be fitted with a deadlock, ie a lock with a bolt that cannot be forced back but has to be turned by a key. There are two forms of deadlock: the *mortice* which is fitted into a hole cut into the door (see page 89) and the *surface-mounted* type (eg **Yale**) which you fix to the inside face of the door. A conventional surface-mounted *nightlatch* does not give adequate protection on its own as it is possible to force it. It should always be fitted in conjunction with a deadlock.

All three types of lock are available from locksmiths and hardware shops.

If you do not feel competent to fit them yourself or are unsure what locks would be best for your home, consult the Crime Prevention Officer at your local police station, your insurance company or a professional locksmith for advice.

It is worth noting that with some deadlocks (including those made by **Ingersoll** and **Chubb**) you can only obtain extra keys by means of a letter with an approved signature to the manufacturer. This means that it is not possible for anyone to get a duplicate key cut and is thus an added security measure.

Remember . . .

An old type of nightlatch can often be replaced with a modern deadlock without requiring many alterations to the door.

The security of a front door relies not only on the lock but also on it being fitted correctly so get a locksmith or carpenter to do the job if you don't feel competent to do it yourself.

Have hinge bolts fitted to doors which open outwards. These prevent would-be burglars from knocking out the hinge pins and removing the door. The bolts are morticed into the hinge side of the door and lock it into the frame.

Garden tools make useful breaking-in implements so keep them locked away in a shed or garage. Similarly, never leave ladders or steps outside. Secure them to a fence or wall with a chain and padlock if it is not possible to lock them away inside.

Insurance companies insist on certain standards of home security, especially if you have valuable possessions, so check that your home complies with your insurers' rules.

Well-lit houses are less likely to be burgled at night, so leave lights on when you go out, and consider installing external lights to illuminate each side of your house.

Milk bottles on the doorstep and newspapers in the letterbox are a clear indication to burglars that a house is temporarily unoccupied, so be sure to cancel all deliveries before you go away.

CARS AND BICYCLES

Unfreezing a car door lock

Do not jam the key into the lock and attempt to force it or you will only bend or break the key. Spray de-icer (available from garage shops and car accessory shops) into the key slot and leave it for a few seconds.

Alternatively, you could try heating the door key with a cigarette lighter or match before putting it in the lock.

It is possible to buy special anti-freeze keys which are left in the lock after the normal key has been used and removed. They cannot be used to unlock the door, but will prevent the lock freezing up.

If you lubricate the lock regularly, it is less likely to freeze up.

Starting a cold engine

Do not continuously work the starter as this will only succeed in flattening the battery and drenching the spark plugs with petrol so that the car will never start. Lift the bonnet and check the spark plugs. If they are damp from condensation, either remove and wipe each plug lead in turn as well as

the distributor cap with a dry rag or give the electrics a spray with **Holts Dampstart** (available from garage shops or car accessory shops). Refer to your car handbook if you are unsure where on the engine these things are.

Coping when a car will not start

If there is no reaction when you turn the ignition key, or the engine just turns sluggishly but does not start, the problem is likely to be the battery. Check by turning on the headlights. If they become dim when you turn on

the ignition, first check that the leads to the battery terminals are clean and correctly connected. If the caps that join the wires to the terminals are dirty or corroded this will prevent electricity flowing.

This can sometimes be cured temporarily (just to enable you to start this time) by tapping the caps lightly with a screwdriver, spanner or other hard object. If this does not work you will need to unscrew the caps and clean them out with a bit of emery paper or the blade of a screwdriver, nail file or other metal item. When you have scraped out all the dirt and corrosion, give the caps a thin smear of **Vaseline** or aerosol lubricant and reconnect them to the correct terminals on the battery. Refer to your car handbook if you are unsure of the position of the battery.

Unblocking car windscreen washers

Use a pin or thin piece of wire to clear the washer nozzles and check that the tubes running from the washer bottle are not kinked or being squashed as this can restrict the flow of water on to the screen. If there is a small mesh washer in the cap of your washer bottle, it may be clogged. Remove it and give it a good wash to clear it.

It is an offence if your washer is not operating, so if you cannot remedy it yourself, have it repaired or replaced by a garage.

Waterproofing a car windscreen

With age, the rubber holding a car windscreen in place either becomes 'tired' and shrinks slightly, or stiff and hard so that it does not accommodate the very slight movement of the windscreen when the car is running. You can usually detect the leaks because of streaks on the glass and water-borne deposits. The rubber goes first at the bottom corners of the screen where the wipers tend to force the water down.

You can sometimes cure the faults with a special screen-sealing compound such as **Holts Screen Sealer** which comes in a tube. With a broad-bladed kitchen knife, gently ease the rubber away from the screen and force the top of the tube between the rubber and the glass. Move the tube slowly along, squeezing the sealer into the gap. Leave for a couple of hours, then trim off excess sealant with a sharp knife.

If this does not work you will need to have the rubber replaced by a professional. Go to your local garage or look under W in the Yellow Pages for a windscreen specialist. Although it is possible to do the job yourself on a car with a fairly flat windscreen, it is tricky and you can run the risk of breaking the glass.

Preventing ice forming on car windows and windscreens

If your car has to stand outside at night, either buy a plastic cover for it or cover the windows with stiff brown paper or several layers of newspaper held in place with masking tape. It is quicker to remove this in the morning than to remove ice from every window. Do not pour hot water over the windows as this could cause the glass to shatter.

Improving faded plastic car seats

Improve the colour by painting with **Humbrol PVC Upholstery Paint** which comes in a wide range of colours from hardware and car accessory shops. Clean the surface thoroughly before applying it.

The treatment will not work on badly worn seats which should be fitted with fabric covers. Where springs have broken, it is best to buy new seats.

Replacing car door seals

When the sealing strips between car doors and bodywork lose their elasticity, water can leak through into the car. Buy replacement sealing strip from a car accessory shop and a special adhesive such as **Bostik Weatherproof Adhesive No. 2** which is quick-drying but allows you time to get the strip into position and make any necessary adjustments.

Clean out the groove, making sure that no old adhesive or bits of rubber are left in it. Check the old strip to see if there are any cuts in it which have been made to negotiate the curves. Make similar cuts in the new strip. Have a dry run without adhesive to make sure that the strip fits exactly and then glue it into place.

Do this job on a dry day or under cover so that you can leave the doors open until the adhesive has set. If you close them too soon the new seals could be displaced.

Brightening up chrome bumpers

Wash with soapy water to remove the worst of the dirt. Attack stubborn marks with a **Brillo pad**, using plenty of water. Mild rusting can be removed with a chrome cleaner or polish such as those made by **Simoniz** and **Holts**. More persistent rust can be removed with a chemical rust remover such as **Kurust**. Dull patches can be brightened with your normal car bodywork polish. Finish off with a rinse of warm water and give a final polish.

Where yellowing has occurred on stainless steel bumpers it is not possible to restore the original colour.

Touching up damaged and rusted sections of car bodywork

Remove any fitting or trim that is near the damaged area. Chip off the loose paint and use coarse wet-and-dry abrasive paper on a block of wood to rub the rusty area down to bare metal. Wet-and-dry abrasive paper is used soaked in water. The water acts as a lubricant so the paper moves easily over the area, and it also prevents dust blowing about. It is available from DIY and car accessory shops.

Dry the area thoroughly with a soft cloth and mask off any nearby trim that could not be removed. With a spray- or brush-on metal primer, such as **Holts**, prime the bare metal. When dry, apply filler, eg **Plastic Padding**, to any dents or pit marks in the metal. Leave the filler until completely dry, then rub it down with wet-and-dry abrasive paper until it is smooth and flush with the paintwork. Dry with a soft cloth and spray on the final coat of paint using an aerosol in a shade to match the rest. (Shake the aerosol thoroughly before spraying.) Use short bursts and make sure you keep the aerosol moving. Leave for at least three weeks before polishing the new paintwork.

Curing fading car headlights

If your headlights fade as you are driving along it is either the fan belt or the battery that is at fault. Check the fan belt and if necessary tighten it. Your car handbook will tell you how to do this but as it's quite difficult and the parts are often hard to get at, this is probably something you should ask your garage to do. If this fails to cure the fading it is likely that your battery is not charging properly. Have it checked at a garage and, if necessary, given a booster charge while you wait, or switch off inessential instruments such as the radio and heated rear window to conserve the battery until you get home.

Always make sure your battery is kept topped up with distilled water. If it is old you will need to check the level as often as you check the water and oil levels in the car. If this problem occurs regularly, it may be that you need a new battery, so get it checked by your garage.

Replacing bicycle handlebar grips

If the old grips are difficult to remove, cut along the underside with a sharp knife, eg a **Stanley** knife, and peel them off. Clean the bare handlebars with abrasive paper to remove rust and old adhesive.

New plastic grips might prove a tight fit and difficult to push on to the handlebars. They will slide on more easily if they are immersed in hot water for a few minutes beforehand.

For grips that are a loose fit, apply a clear adhesive such as **Bostik 1** or **UHU** to the insides of the grips and slide them on to the handlebars. Allow the adhesive to dry before using the bicycle.

Checking a valve on a bicycle tyre

Turn the wheel round until the valve is at the bottom and screw the flexible tube from your bicycle pump on to the valve. Place the end of the flexible tube into a jam jar full of water. If the valve is leaking, you will see air bubbling up from the end of the tube.

Modern bicycles usually have a spring-loaded valve which will have to be completely replaced. The old type can be repaired by replacing the rubber tube on the stem of the valve. Both are available from car and bicycle accessory shops.

Replacing worn brake blocks

Apart from being dangerous, riding a bicycle with ineffective brakes is an offence against the Road Traffic Act, so you should regularly check that your brakes are working properly.

If the brake blocks are worn, new ones can be bought from bicycle shops. Take the old ones with you to be sure of getting the right replacements. Unscrew the nut holding the brake shoes and remove them completely, then lever out the worn rubber block with an old screwdriver.

Slide the new rubber blocks into the brake shoes and replace the brake shoes, making sure that the closed ends of the shoes face the direction of travel of the bicycle if you have

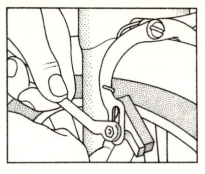

caliper (cable) brakes. For other types of brake, check with your local bicycle repair shop.

Complete sets of brake shoes and blocks can be bought. This saves the trouble of levering out worn blocks.

Adjusting a loose bicycle chain

This problem should be dealt with immediately otherwise an accident could be caused if the chain jumps off. Adjustment should be made if the chain has more than 19 mm of up-and-down slack at the point midway between the chain wheel and the rear sprocket.

Slacken off the nuts on the rear wheel spindle and move the wheel backwards in the forks until tension is

applied to the chain. Tighten the nuts up carefully, making sure the wheel remains central between the forks, and give the nuts a final tightening up. Reverse this procedure if the chain is too tight.

If you cannot adjust the chain by this method, you will need to have a link taken out. A bicycle repair shop will do this for you.

Tightening up bicycle lamp brackets

The brackets holding front and rear lamps frequently become loose and out of adjustment so that they cannot be seen clearly by other road users.

Remove the lamps from the brackets and tighten up the locking ring on the front bracket with a spanner. Hold the bracket firmly to

make sure it faces forward. The rear light is usually fixed to a clamp-type bracket which can be tightened up and realigned using a screwdriver and spanner.

Before replacing the lamps, clean up the glass and check that they are working properly.

Remember . . .

When using an aerosol paint to touch up a car body repair, choose a dry, still day if you have to work outside. Aerosol paints tend to drift so mask adjacent areas of bodywork and equipment whether working inside or out.

Aerosol paints need shaking up in the can to mix them thoroughly. It is better to apply several thin coats than one thick one.

Cars and bicycles usually need different sizes of spanners. It is well worth investing in a suitable set with all the sizes you need if you plan to do small maintenance jobs yourself.

Never let oil or grease get into the rims of bicycle wheels as this will make the brakes slip.

When buying a new bicycle, go to a reputable cycle dealer displaying the National Cycling Proficiency Scheme window sign or the sign of the National Association of Cycle Traders. Contact the Association by telephone on Tunbridge Wells (0892) 26081 for the address of your local branch secretary who will be able to tell you about members in your vicinity.

STAIN REMOVAL

SAFETY WARNING

Many stain removing agents, including proprietary products, are potentially harmful if not actually poisonous. Some are highly flammable; others give off toxic fumes.

The sensible course is to treat all stain removing substances with caution and, in the case of proprietary products, to follow the manufacturers' directions scrupulously. Observe the following simple rules as a routine measure:

When using Always work in a well-ventilated room, preferably with the window open. Never use stain removing agents in a room where there is a naked flame, pilot light or radiant heater. Never smoke while working with, or anywhere near to, stain removing agents. Do not decant the solvent into another container. Wear rubber gloves.

When storing Keep all the items in your stain removing kit out of the reach of children or elderly people whose sight is failing, or who may become confused; best of all, keep your kit locked away. Never put away anything that is not clearly labelled. Store—and indeed buy—small quantities only of all stain removing substances. Take extra precautions when using or handling:

Methylated spirit	Highly flammable and poisonous
Spirits of salts	Poisonous and corrosive
Amyl acetate *Liquid lighter fuel* *Turpentine* *White spirit, or turpentine substitute* *Non-oily nail varnish remover* *Cellulose thinners*	Flammable and dangerous to inhale; poisonous
Ammonia	Unpleasant fumes; avoid contact with eyes, skin or clothing; poisonous

GENERAL INFORMATION

It's usually much easier to remove a stain if you deal with it as soon as it occurs, unless it requires professional treatment. It is essential, whatever method of removal you adopt, to test it first on a small hidden area of the surface.

There are a number of quick first-aid treatments which are useful if for some reason you are prevented from dealing thoroughly with the stain immediately. Non-greasy stains can be sponged or rinsed in cold water. Greasy stains can be sprinkled with talcum powder to stop them spreading. Salt thrown on wine, fruit or beetroot stains on fabrics will stop them spreading, but this measure should not be taken on carpets as the salt tends to affect colours and to leave a damp patch which is more susceptible to soiling.

One golden rule is to go cautiously when treating all stains. Milder methods repeated as often as necessary are far more effective than a blast from a strong solvent which is more likely to damage the surface than remove the stain.

When working on a stain, treat a ring around the stain and then work from the outside to the middle: this prevents it from spreading. It is also important to dab at a stain rather than rub it: this may spread the stain and damage the surface. Always use white absorbent cotton cloth or cotton wool for a dabber. The dyes in a coloured fabric dabber may be affected by certain solvents and result in you having to deal with two stains instead of just one!

Professional cleaning is a must if you have a difficult stain on an expensive fabric or piece of soft furnishing. Although expensive, it will certainly pay off in terms of saving the item from permanent damage. Professional dry cleaners have a battery of cleaning solvents not available on the domestic market and they should be able to deal with even the most obstinate stains. It is best not to attempt home treatment first as this can complicate matters and sometimes make it impossible for the cleaners to remove the stain. Be sure to tell the cleaners exactly what has been spilled and also to confess if you have had a go yourself.

An *absorbed stain* may respond to squeezing in lukewarm suds followed by laundering but it is important not to use hot water as this might set the stain. Sponging with clear warm water is the best treatment for dry-clean-only fabrics, unless of course they watermark. Blot well with a clean towel. Remember that a stain has fallen *on* to something and therefore needs to be taken *off* it. When applying a solvent to an absorbed stain that has not responded to sponging or laundering, work from the side underneath the stain, if possible, holding a dry white absorbent pad on the other side.

A *built-up stain*, ie a stain resulting from spillage of a thicker preparation such as grease, nail varnish or paint, does not generally penetrate far into the surface. Act quickly to remove as much of the deposit as possible with paper tissues, towels or a scraper such as the back of a knife blade. It is best to treat any remaining stain from the underside, where possible, with a pad held on top of the mark so that the deposit is not driven through the fabric. Any absorbent pad used in this way should be moved around continually to prevent any of the stain being redeposited on the surface.

A *compound stain* is a combination of the two mentioned above. Blood, for example, penetrates the surface but also leaves a residue on top. First the surface deposit should be dealt with as for a built-up stain and then the penetration should be attended to as for an absorbed stain. Any traces can usually be cleared with laundering and sponging.

Upholstery and carpets

Don't over-wet upholstered furniture or carpets. It helps to blot up with an old towel as you go along. Be particularly careful not to over-wet acrylic velvet (eg Dralon) which is woven on to either a cotton or a cotton/synthetic mixture backing which could shrink and distort the surface.

Water-borne stains can often be removed from Dralon velvet and non-removable flat-weave Dralon covers by immediate and thorough blotting followed, where necessary, by sprinkling the stain with a weak warm solution of biological detergent (5 ml detergent to 1 litre of water) and lightly wiping in the direction of the pile with a sponge. Velvets other than acrylic should be treated professionally.

On carpets, a squirt from a soda syphon will flush out spilled liquids if used immediately the spill occurs. Dirty marks and water-soluble stains can usually be removed with carpet shampoo. Treat the stain itself with the carpet shampoo, then shampoo the entire carpet if necessary to avoid a conspicuously clean patch.

Where a carpet can be lifted, treat the back as well, but take great care with solvents on rubber-latexed or foam-backed carpets.

Following treatment, smooth the carpet pile in the direction in which it lies and allow it to dry naturally— never apply artificial heat, this could damage it—before replacing the furniture.

For water-based stains, if you have run out of shampoo, use a solution of 5 ml washing up detergent and 5 ml white vinegar to 1 litre of warm water.

The stain remover's kit

Listed here are a few of the useful items to have handy in case of accidents. Remember that the majority of the substances are *poisonous* and should be kept locked away out of the reach of children. Some of the solvents are also *highly flammable*, and some give off *toxic vapours*. Ensure good ventilation in the room where you are working with them, don't smoke, extinguish all naked flames (even pilot lights) and wear rubber gloves to protect your hands.

Biological washing powder Effective as a pre-wash soak for protein stains such as blood, egg yolk, milk, gravy. It should not be used on wool, silk or on non-colour-fast, flame-resistant or rubberised fabrics.

Glycerine Useful for lubricating and softening staining substances. Dilute in equal parts with warm water. Rub into the fabric and leave for one hour. Remove by rinsing or sponging with lukewarm water.

Grease solvents Proprietary grease solvents, hereafter called stain removers, remove grease and oil marks and some will also cope with other stains. Follow the manufacturer's instructions exactly. Good ones include **Boots Dry Cleaner**, **Beaucaire**, **Thawpit** and **Dabitoff** liquids, **Goddard's Dry Clean** and **K2r** aerosols and **K2r** paste.

Household ammonia Good for neutralising acid marks. Dilute with at least 3 parts of water. Avoid contact with skin, eyes and clothing.

Hydrogen peroxide Available from chemists, this is a mild, slow-acting, oxidising bleach. Buy it in 20-vol strength and use it diluted with 6 parts of cold water. It should not be used on nylon or flame-resistant fabrics, though most other fabrics, including silk, can be soaked in the solution for up to 30 minutes.

Laundry or domestic borax A mild alkali which works on acid stains. Usually used in a solution of 15 ml to 500 ml warm water for sponging or for soaking washable fabrics (10–15 minutes). Can be used safely on most fabrics.

Methylated spirit Highly *flammable* and *poisonous*. Use it neat, dabbed on to the stain, but check first that the colour will not be affected. Never use on acetate or triacetate fabrics or on French-polished surfaces where it will dissolve the polish.

White vinegar or dilute acetic acid Thoroughly rinse it out after treating the fabric for stains. Never use on acetate or triacetate fabrics and take care not to get it on your skin.

Other solvents The following are all useful solvents to keep in your kit—nearly all *flammable* and *dangerous to inhale*: amyl acetate, white spirit or turpentine substitute, liquid lighter fuel, non-oily nail varnish remover (don't use on acetate or triacetate fabrics) and cellulose thinners.

Pre-wash aerosols For use on heavily soiled and stained areas on washable, colour-fast fabrics. Two examples are **Frend** and **Shout**. They break down most types of staining matter so that the residue can be washed out by the normal laundering process. This eliminates the need for pre-soaking, hard rubbing, scrubbing or boiling.

They are most effective when used on dry fabric, immediately before laundering, and work best on grease-based soiling and fresh stains.

Proprietary kits These are designed to cope with most household stains and usually contain a number of small bottles of different chemicals which you use individually or mix together according to the stain. Good ones include the **ServiceMaster First Aid Kit** for carpets, rugs and furniture and **Holloway's Carpet Care Spot Removing Kit**.

REMOVING STAINS

Adhesives
Scrape off the deposit, then treat as follows according to type.

Clear adhesives eg Bostik No. 1, UHU
On carpets Dab any stain lightly with a pad and non-oily nail varnish remover. If you're not sure what the pile is made of, use amyl acetate but check first for dye bleeding.

On upholstery Where possible, hold an absorbent pad on the right side and work from the wrong side, dabbing with a pad and non-oily nail varnish remover. On acetate and triacetate, use amyl acetate but check first for dye bleeding.

Contact adhesive eg Evo-Stik
On carpets As for *clear adhesives*. If you're not sure what the pile is made of, you could try lighter fuel or amyl acetate.

On upholstery As for *clear adhesives*. On acetate and triacetate, use lighter fuel or amyl acetate. Check first for dye bleeding.

Epoxy resin adhesive eg Araldite
On carpets Dab with cellulose thinners. On a synthetic pile carpet or a synthetic fibre mixture, use lighter fuel. Dried stains will be impossible to remove but trimming the pile with sharp scissors will remove a light surface deposit.

On upholstery Where possible, hold a pad over the deposit and dab from

Check first with safety rules on page 98

the wrong side with cellulose thinners. On synthetic fibres, use lighter fuel. Stains that have dried will be impossible to remove.

Latex adhesive eg Copydex
On carpets Scrape off surface deposit with the back of a knife blade. The makers of **Copydex** produce a special solvent which will remove the stain.
On upholstery While still wet, this can be removed with a damp cloth. Once dry, scrape off the deposit and dab the remaining stain with the manufacturer's solvent. The paint-brush cleaner **Polyclens Plus** will also clear the stain. Do not use paint strippers as they usually contain chemicals which may damage fabrics.
On hard surfaces Gentle rubbing with a clean fingertip will usually roll off latex adhesive, unless it has been allowed to set for some time.

Model-making cement eg Humbrol Polystyrene Cement
On carpets and upholstery Wipe off as much as possible, taking care not to spread the adhesive. Dab the remainder with a pad well moistened with liquid stain remover. Once dried, the cement is extremely difficult to remove but some manufacturers produce a solvent.

Animal stains
Excreta/urine/sick on carpets Remove deposit with absorbent paper or a spoon. Flush the area with a squirt from a soda syphon, or sponge with clear, warm water. Blot dry. Use a proprietary pet stain remover to clear and deodorise the area, eg **Shaws Pet Stain Remover**. Finally, shampoo the area, if necessary. Blot well. Dried matter can sometimes be softened for easier removal by using a proprietary pet stain remover.

Urine/sick on upholstery Remove any deposit with absorbent paper, taking care not to spread the mark. If it is not possible to remove the upholstery item, try to isolate the affected area by gathering up the fabric and tying white tape or string tightly round it. Rinse under cold running water if possible, or use a pet stain remover. Launder or sponge and allow to dry naturally.

Beer
On carpets Flush fresh stains with a squirt from a soda syphon, or sponge with clear warm water. Blot well. Treat any remaining stain or dried marks with a solution of carpet shampoo, eg **1001 Dri-Foam**. Alternatively, use a proprietary spotting kit, eg **Holloway's Carpet Care Spot Removing Kit**. Gentle sponging with methylated spirit may reduce old stains.
On upholstery Blot well and wipe with a cloth wrung out in clear, luke-warm water. Dried stains on non-acetate/triacetate fabrics should be sponged carefully with a white vinegar solution (1 part white vinegar to 5 parts water) and then with clear water. Blot well. Alternatively, and for acetate or triacetate fabrics, sponge with clear water. Blot well, then allow to dry naturally, and treat with a proprietary aerosol cleaner such as **K2r Stain Remover Spray** or **Goddard's Dry Clean**.

Blood
On carpets Flush out fresh stains with a squirt from a soda syphon, or sponge well with cold water. Blot dry. If necessary, shampoo the affected area. Alternatively, use a proprietary carpet spot removal treat-ment. It may not be possible to clear dried stains.
On mattresses Tip the mattress on to its side and, pressing a towel beneath

the stained area to avoid spreading the mark, sponge with cold salt water, then clear cold water. The lather from an upholstery shampoo is usually effective on fresh marks and may also clear dried stains. Treating mattress stains is done more easily by two people—one to hold and one to dab. Mattress covers may ring-mark but this is preferable to an untreated stain.

On upholstery Wipe or brush lightly to remove any surface deposit. Sponge with cold water to which you have added a few drops of ammonia (2.5 ml to every 1 litre). Rinse with clear water and blot well. Alternatively, use an upholstery spotting kit.

Butter *see* Fats, grease and oils

Candlewax
On carpets Scrape off as much as possible of the deposit with the bowl of a spoon. To melt the remainder, place a sheet of blotting paper or brown paper over it and gently apply the toe of a warm iron to the mark. Do not let the iron touch the pile, which would probably scorch or melt, and keep moving the paper around until all the wax is absorbed. Clear remaining wax with a stain remover. Remove any remaining colour by dabbing with methylated spirit.

On upholstery On closely woven fabrics, melt out the wax with a moderately hot iron over clean blotting paper. Remove any remaining colour by dabbing with methylated spirit (not on acetate or triacetate). On loosely woven fabrics do not attempt to pull off any wax or you may pull threads. Melt it out with an iron and blotting paper. On pile fabrics, it is often possible to remove the deposit by rubbing lightly with a cloth. Otherwise use the iron and

blotting paper treatment with blotting paper on the pile side and the iron applied to the back. Where this is not possible, hold the iron over the blotting paper but without depressing the pile. Clear any traces of wax with an aerosol stain remover, eg **Goddard's Dry Clean**.

On vinyl wall coverings Wait until the wax hardens, then lift it off carefully, dabbing gently with methylated spirit to remove any remaining colour. A liquid household cleaner, eg **Handy Andy**, should remove any slight stain remaining.

On wallpaper Do not attempt to lift the wax or scrape the paper which will tear away, leaving holes. Use a warm iron over a sheet of blotting paper to melt and absorb the wax. Keep moving the blotting paper around to expose clear surfaces. If a stain remains, use an aerosol stain remover, eg **K2r**. Sometimes it may not be possible to remove all traces.

Car and cycle oil
On concrete drives and garage floors Use **Polyclens Plus** paintbrush cleaner. This product is not suitable for asphalt surfaces.

Chewing gum
On carpets and upholstery Use **Holloway Chewing Gum Remover**. This is an aerosol which freezes the deposit so that it can be broken up and brushed clear. Follow the maker's instructions, test an area first, then apply with care as it reaches a low temperature in use and could burn the skin. Brush up the deposit by hand as the bits could gum up a vacuum cleaner.

Chocolate
On carpets and upholstery Scrape off as much as possible with the back

Check first with safety rules on page 98

of a knife blade. Treat the stained area of a carpet with carpet shampoo. Treat stains on upholstery and any remaining carpet stain with a liquid stain remover, eg **Beaucaire**.

Cocoa

On carpets Spoon and blot up as much as possible. Flush out the stain with a squirt from a soda syphon, or sponge with warm water. Blot well. Use a carpet shampoo or a carpet spotting kit. When dry, remove any traces with a liquid stain remover, eg **Beaucaire**. Dried stains should be sponged well with a laundry borax solution (15 ml borax to 500 ml warm water). Blot dry and, if a mark remains, rub in a mixture of equal parts of glycerine and warm water. Leave for up to an hour then rinse and blot. Repeat the borax treatment if necessary.

On upholstery Sponge with a laundry borax solution (15 ml borax to 500 ml warm water), then with clear water. Blot dry. Clear any traces when dry by applying a stain remover, eg **K2r**. Alternatively, use an upholstery spotting kit.

Coffee

On carpets Spoon and blot up as much as possible. Flush out the stain with a squirt from a soda syphon, or sponge with warm water and blot dry. This will probably deal with fresh black coffee stains. For remaining marks and white coffee, use a carpet shampoo or a carpet spot removal kit. When dry, remove any final traces with a stain remover, eg **Beaucaire**. Dried coffee stains may respond to repeated flushing from a soda syphon. Allow time to dry between each application.

On upholstery Treat as for **Cocoa**. Coffee stains on acrylic velvet, eg Dralon, should be thoroughly blotted with tissue or a cloth. Sprinkle any

remaining stain with a warm solution of biological washing powder (5 ml powder to 1 litre water) and rub lightly with a sponge in the direction of the pile. This avoids over-wetting. Flat-weave Dralons can be similarly treated. Old stains should be lubricated with a glycerine solution (equal parts glycerine and warm water), left for up to an hour, then rinsed with a cloth wrung out in warm water. Blot well.

Crayon

On vinyl wallcoverings A wipe with a damp cloth may be sufficient. If not, use a household cleaner, eg **Handy Andy**.

On wallpaper There is no treatment for this. Tear, not cut, another piece of wallpaper to cover the area and paste it over (see page 11). On dense patterns this should give a fairly invisible mend, though it will tend to show on plain papers.

Cream (edible) *see* **Fats, grease and oils**

Curry

On carpets Scrape up any deposit and rub the stain lightly with a cloth wrung out in a solution of laundry borax (15 ml borax to 500 ml warm water). If this fails, rub a little neat glycerine into the carpet pile, leave for about 10 minutes, then sponge out with warm water. Blot dry. This is a difficult stain and large marks should be cleaned professionally.

Dyes

On floors It is essential to wipe up splashes or spills immediately with a dry absorbent cloth. Avoid the use of water. There is no remedy for dried stains.

On carpets and upholstery Carefully sponge with methylated spirit (not acetate or triacetate fabrics) to which you have added a few drops of household ammonia. Alternatively and more safely, have the items dry cleaned professionally.

Egg
On carpets Remove as much of the deposit as possible with a dry cloth or by scraping. Treat with a liquid stain remover, eg **Beaucaire**, followed where necessary by a carpet shampoo. Alternatively, use a carpet spotting kit.
On upholstery Scrape off the surface deposit. Sponge egg white with cold salt water, then clear water. Blot dry. Use **K2r Stain Remover** if necessary. On egg yolk, work in the lather from a washing-up detergent solution or upholstery shampoo. Wipe with a damp cloth. When dry, use a liquid stain remover if necessary. For whole egg, use a stain remover or upholstery spotting kit.

Fats, grease and oils
On carpets Blot up or scrape off deposit. Apply a stain remover, eg **Beaucaire** or **Boots Dry Cleaner**. Take particular care where there is a foam or rubber-latexed backing. For heavy deposits use an iron and blotting paper as described for **Candlewax**. When no more grease can be removed, brush or rub in the lather from a solution of carpet shampoo, eg **Bissell**, or use an aerosol foam carpet cleaner, eg **Johnson Glory**. Traces of the deposit may continue to creep up (called "wicking back" in the trade) for some time and you may need to repeat the application.
On leather upholstery Cover the stain with a thin layer of bicycle puncture repair adhesive. An initial test on a small area is essential since most adhesives contain colouring matter which could stain lighter shades. Leave for 24 hours, then roll off carefully—it should have

absorbed the grease. Treat the article with a good quality hide food, eg **Hidelife, Cee Bee Hide Food**.
On upholstery Spread French chalk, talcum powder or powdered starch over a small mark. Replace when it becomes impregnated with oil. Leave for several hours, then brush clear. Alternatively, use a proprietary stain remover such as **Beaucaire** or **Boots Dry Cleaner**. Take care with foam backings. Grease on flat-woven and velvet-pile Dralon should be treated with **Thawpit** or **Dabitoff**. For larger areas (though not on Dralon or other pile fabrics), press with a warm iron over clean blotting paper to absorb the deposit, and finally apply a stain remover, eg **Beaucaire**.
On wallpaper Use a warm iron over clean blotting paper to draw out as much grease as possible. **K2r Stain Remover**, in either aerosol or paste form, can be used to clear remaining marks. For hessian wallcovering, use an aerosol stain remover, eg **K2r Stain Remover**, very sparingly and check first for dye change as fairly weak colours are used in hessians.

Foundation cream
On upholstery Wipe up any wet deposit carefully. Brush a dried stain with a soft brush to clear any powder. Apply an aerosol stain remover, eg **K2r**, for fabrics which might ringmark with liquids. Alternatively, talcum powder or French chalk can be rubbed into light-coloured fabrics. After 2 hours shake and brush lightly with a soft-bristled brush. An upholstery spotting kit may also be used.

Fruit juice
On carpets Scoop up and absorb as much as possible with paper towels. Shampoo the area and, when dry,

Check first with safety rules on page 98

remove any remaining traces by dabbing with a cloth moistened in methylated spirit.
On upholstery Sponge with cold water and blot dry. Use an upholstery stain removal kit or a **Spotkleen** impregnated cleaning cloth.

Gin and other spirits
On carpets Blot up excess fluid and flush the mark with a squirt from a soda syphon, or sponge with a cloth lightly wrung out in warm water. Blot well. If staining remains, apply the lather of a carpet shampoo, eg **Bissell**. Alternatively, use a carpet spotting kit. Sponging with methylated spirit may reduce old stains.
On upholstery Sponge with clear lukewarm water, then blot dry. If staining remains, apply the lather from an upholstery shampoo solution or washing-up detergent. Rub lightly, then wipe clear with a cloth wrung out in warm water and blot dry. Alternatively, use an upholstery spotting kit.

Gravy
On carpets Scoop up excess and wipe with a dry cloth to remove as much as possible. Treat with a liquid stain remover, eg **Boots Dry Cleaner**, followed by a carpet shampoo. Alternatively, use a carpet spotting kit.
On upholstery Treat with a stain remover, eg **Beaucaire**. Wipe with a cloth wrung out in warm water provided the fabric doesn't watermark.

Hair oil
On fabric-upholstered headboards Treat with a stain remover, eg **Thawpit** or **Dabitoff** (both especially recommended for Dralons), or **Goddard's Dry Clean**. Do not over-apply, particularly on padded areas. Avoid marks recurring by treating the

headboard with a protective spray, eg **Scotchgard Fabric Protector**.
On wooden headboards Rub with a cloth moistened in white spirit. Buff well with a soft dry cloth.
On wallcoverings Hessian and wallpaper—treat as for **Fats, grease and oils** on hessian wallcoverings. Washable wallpaper—Sponge the mark with a warm, well-diluted washing-up detergent solution. Rinse with a cloth wrung out in clear water and pat dry.
On vinyl—Wipe gently with a cloth wrung out in a solution of general purpose household cleaner and rinse. Stubborn marks should be rubbed lightly with white spirit.
Painted walls—Wipe the area gently with a general purpose household cleaner used neat. Dab with a cloth wrung out in clear water.

Ice cream
On carpets Scrape up the deposit and wipe with a damp cloth to remove as much of the staining as possible. Apply a carpet shampoo. Alternatively, use a carpet spotting kit.
On upholstery Wipe off surface deposit. Sponge with lukewarm water. When dry, treat any remaining stain with a stain remover, eg **Beaucaire**. Remaining traces can be bleached out carefully with a hydrogen peroxide solution (1 part 20-vol peroxide to 6 parts cold water) if the fabric is suitable (not nylon).

Ink

Ballpoint
On upholstery Act quickly or the stain may become impossible to remove. Most types respond to light dabbing with methylated spirit on a cotton wool bud. If a test section proves unsuccessful, contact the pen manufacturer for advice.

On vinyl upholstery and wall-coverings Unless treated immediately this stain cannot be removed as the ink quickly merges into the plasticiser and causes permanent marking. Treatment is to scrub at once with a nail brush, using warm water and soap or detergent.

Felt-tip

On upholstery Small marks should be dabbed with methylated spirit on a cotton wool bud (never use on acetate or triacetate materials). If it is not possible to launder, use the aerosol stain remover **K2r**.

On vinyl bedheads and wallcoverings Carefully use a household cleaner, eg **Handy Andy**, or methylated spirit. If these fail, use neat washing-up liquid applied on a cloth over one finger. Finish with a car vinyl cleaner, eg **Turtle Wax Upholstery Cleaner**.

Fountain-pen ink

On carpets Flush with a squirt from a soda syphon, then blot with absorbent paper. Remove as much further ink as possible by sponging with warm water, blotting to avoid over-wetting. Apply a small quantity of dry foam carpet shampoo. Repeat as necessary, blotting well between applications. Any small stains remaining on light-coloured carpets can be treated with a solution of sodium hydrosulphite (obtainable in powder form from some chemists), using 25 ml sodium hydrosulphite to 600 ml water. Do a test first as it has a bleaching action. If satisfactory, apply small amounts, blotting between each. Rinse with warm water. Alternatively, use a carpet spotting kit after initial blotting. Old stains usually require professional treatment, though if you know the type of ink spilt, the manufacturer may be able to suggest a process.

On upholstery Treat fresh stains on upholstery with an upholstery spotting kit. If this is not available, sponge gently with cold water and blot well to remove as much as possible. When dry, follow with repeated applications of a stain remover, eg **K2r** aerosol, to clear any traces. For loose covers, sponge with cold water until no more ink can be removed. Launder if possible to clear traces. If marks remain after laundering, squeeze lemon juice over them and press the stained area between two pieces of white cotton cloth. Repeat as necessary, then rinse thoroughly.

Jam, marmalade

On carpets Scoop up and wipe off any surface deposit with a cloth wrung out in warm water. Treat the area with a carpet shampoo or use a carpet spotting kit. Any fruit colour remaining should respond to dabbing with methylated spirit.

On upholstery Wipe off any surface deposit. Sponge the stain with a cloth moistened in a warm solution of washing-up liquid. If marks persist, rub on a little laundry borax powder, leave for a few minutes, then sponge clear. Alternatively, use an upholstery spotting kit or sponge the stain with clear warm water, allow to dry and apply **K2r Stain Remover**.

Ketchup and other bottled sauces

On carpets Scoop and wipe up excess with a clean damp cloth, being careful not to spread the stain. Dried stains can sometimes be softened by rubbing in a glycerine solution (equal parts glycerine and warm water). Leave for about 20 minutes, then sponge with clear warm water, blotting to avoid over-wetting. Gently rub lather from a whisked-up solution of carpet

Check first with safety rules on page 98

shampoo on to any remaining stain. Wipe in the direction of the pile with a cloth wrung out in lukewarm water. When dry, repeated applications of an aerosol stain remover, eg **K2r**, should clear any traces.
On upholstery Scrape carefully with the back of a knife blade to remove excess. Wipe lightly with a clean damp cloth. Apply an aerosol stain remover, eg **K2r**, when the fabric has dried. Professional treatment is advised for tomato-based sauces and delicate fabrics.

Lipstick
On carpets Scrape carefully with the back of a knife blade to remove any surface deposit, then treat with a stain remover such as **Polyclens Plus** paintbrush cleaner or a carpet spot removal kit. Clear indelible lipstick colour by careful application of methylated spirit.
On gloss- or emulsion-painted walls and vinyl wallcoverings Rub the marks lightly with a damp cloth or one wrung out in a warm detergent solution. Stubborn marks may respond to a cream-type household cleaner, eg **Jif**.
On upholstery Dab gently with eucalyptus oil or use a liquid stain remover such as **Boots Dry Cleaner**.
On wallpaper **K2r Stain Remover**, in aerosol or paste form, can be used on this. Stubborn marks and indelible lipstick may need to be covered by a new piece of wallpaper (see page 11).

Metal polish
On carpets Spoon and blot up as much as possible. Dab the area with white spirit. Use a stiff carpet brush to clear the powdery deposit when the pile has dried. Shampoo if necessary. Dried stains should be brushed before treatment is applied. The manufacturers of **Brasso** produce a solvent for its removal.

On upholstery Wipe with a tissue to clear as much of the deposit as possible. Apply a stain remover such as **Boots Dry Cleaner**. Laundering should remove traces from removable washable fabrics. On non-washable fabrics, sponge off as much as possible and brush well when dry. Treat any remaining marks with an aerosol stain remover. The solvent available for **Brasso** on carpets can also be used on fabrics.

Milk
On carpets Speedy treatment is vital to stop penetration and drying, otherwise the smell is virtually impossible to eradicate. Use a soda syphon or lukewarm water to flush the area well, then blot thoroughly. Next use a carpet shampoo or carpet spot removal kit. If a stain remains when the carpet is dry, apply a stain remover, eg **Beaucaire**, but do not allow it to soak on to a rubber-latexed or foam backing. Although it may be possible to remove dried stains yourself, professional cleaning may still be necessary to clear the smell which becomes apparent whenever the room warms up.
On upholstery Sponge with luke-warm water. If a stain remains when the fabric is dry, use a stain remover, eg **Goddard's Dry Clean** or **Thawpit** (recommended for use on Dralons). Alternatively, use an upholstery spotting kit.

Mud
On carpets Allow the mud to dry completely, then brush off with a stiff-bristled carpet brush. Vacuum the carpet, then use a carpet shampoo, eg **Bissell**, **Johnson Glory**, or a carpet spotting kit. Any colour traces that remain should be dabbed lightly with methylated spirit.
On upholstery Allow the mud to dry completely, then lightly brush it off.

Sponge any remaining marks with a warm, mild detergent solution. Wipe with a cloth wrung out in clear water and blot well.

Nail varnish

On carpets Carefully scoop and wipe up as much of the deposit as possible with a spoon and paper tissues, trying to avoid spreading the stain. Dab the mark with a pad of cotton wool moistened with amyl acetate, after testing near the edge of the carpet. A pad soaked with non-oily nail varnish remover can also be used following an initial test. Over-soaking with these solvents could damage carpet backings. Alternatively, use a carpet spotting kit. Any remaining colour should respond to dabbing with methylated spirit. Finish by applying an aerosol carpet shampoo, or the lather of a carpet shampoo solution to the treated area.

On upholstery Wipe up spills immediately, using absorbent paper or cotton wool. Where possible, hold a white absorbent pad beneath the stain and dab with amyl acetate (safe on most fabrics but an initial test is advised). A pad moistened with non-oily nail varnish remover can also be used, but not on acetates and tri-acetates. Any colour remaining can usually be cleared by dabbing with methylated spirit but this should never be used on acetate or triacetate. Launder the fabric where possible. Heavy spills on acetate or triacetate need professional cleaning.

Paints

General note

More recently-developed types of paint, where cleaning the brushes in a washing-up liquid solution is recommended by manufacturers, can usually be removed from most surfaces by laundering or sponging

immediately (don't wait until you've finished the painting job). It is essential in fact to treat all paint spills speedily as dried paint marks of any kind are very difficult to remove. With all paint spills, first scrape and wipe off as much as possible and then treat according to type.

Emulsion and water-based undercoat

Treat wet paint by sponging immediately with cold water, taking care to mop carefully round the edges to avoid spreading the stain. Launder in warm suds where possible. With dried emulsion stains, use methylated spirit to soften the deposit but take care that it does not affect any colour (do not use on acetate or triacetate). Alternatively, use **Polyclens Plus** paintbrush cleaner. Follow by laundering or sponging. Delicate fabrics and large areas of dried emulsion on upholstery or carpets are best treated professionally.

Gloss (oil-based) and oil-based undercoat

Dab carefully with white spirit or **Polyclens Plus** paintbrush cleaner after an initial test. Sponge with cold water and repeat the treatment if necessary. Launder where possible; shampoo carpets and upholstery. Alternatively, use a carpet or upholstery spotting kit. Treat dried stains with a paintbrush cleaner or, as a last resort, a chemical paint remover. Test first. Bad marks need professional treatment.

Paraffin oil

On carpets Do not smoke as paraffin is *highly flammable*. Tackle the mark at once as oil which penetrates to the back of a carpet can cause dye seepage and deterioration of foam or rubber-latexed backing. Mop up as

Check first with safety rules on page 98

much as possible with absorbent
paper or rags, then use an aerosol
stain remover, eg **Goddard's Dry
Clean** or **K2r**, repeating applications
until the mark clears.
On upholstery Treat as for **Fats,
grease and oils**.

Plasticine
On carpets and upholstery Carefully
scrape off as much as possible. Hold
an absorbent pad under the stain, if
possible, and dab it with a liquid stain
remover, eg **Thawpit** or **Dabitoff**, to
dissolve the deposit. On small areas,
dabbing with liquid lighter fuel may
do the trick but this needs care on
synthetic fabrics. Avoid dampening
the carpet backing. Washable fabrics
should then be laundered as usual,
and non-washable should be
sponged gently with warm water and
blotted dry at once.

Rust marks
On carpets and upholstery Use a
proprietary rust stain remover, eg
Magica, following the manufacturer's
instructions.

Scorch marks
On carpets Where scorching is slight
it may be possible to trim the tufts
with scissors. Otherwise, use a stiff-
bristled brush to remove any
loosened fibres. Then take a wire
brush or piece of coarse glasspaper
and make gentle circular movements
to hide the area. Some carpet retailers
are prepared to re-tuft or patch
damaged areas but this is an
expensive job to have done.
On upholstery On non-washable
fabrics, use a glycerine solution
(equal parts glycerine and warm
water) to lubricate light marks, leave
for up to an hour, then sponge with
warm water. On heavier marks,
sponge with a cloth wrung out in a
laundry borax solution (15 ml borax

to 500 ml warm water). Rinse and
repeat the treatment if necessary,
blotting well to avoid over-wetting.
On washable fabrics, light marks
should be rubbed, fabric to fabric,
under cold running water, then
soaked in a warm laundry borax
solution (15 ml borax to 500 ml
warm water) until clear. Rinse and
launder as usual. Heavy marks cannot
usually be removed completely,
although those on white fabrics,
except nylon, will sometimes respond
to careful bleaching with a hydrogen
peroxide solution (1 part 20-vol
peroxide to 6 parts cold water).

Shellac
On upholstery Act quickly before it
has a chance to dry and harden. Dab
lightly with a cotton wool pad
moistened with methylated spirit (not
on acetate or triacetate fabrics). On
non-washable fabrics, follow by
wiping with a cloth wrung out in a
warm synthetic detergent solution.
Finish with clear water and blot well.
Professional treatment will be
necessary for delicate fabrics and
dried stains. On washable fabrics it
may be possible to soften the dried
shellac sufficiently with methylated
spirit so that any remaining deposit
and colour can be laundered or
sponged out with a synthetic
detergent solution.

Shoe polish
On carpets Scrape off as much of the
deposit as possible. Dab either with a
stain remover or white spirit to
dissolve any remaining particles. If
any stain remains, dab with
methylated spirit and finally shampoo
the treated area. Alternatively, treat
the mark with a carpet spotting kit
after scraping off the deposit.
On upholstery Scrape off as much of
the deposit as possible. On non-
washable fabrics, treat as for carpets

and finish off by sponging with warm water then blotting dry. On washable fabrics, use a liquid stain remover or **Polyclens Plus** to remove the mark, or use a few drops of ammonia in the water when laundering. Heavy marking should respond to treatment with **Polyclens Plus** or white spirit. Rinse. Launder where possible.

Smoke and soot

On brickwork Use a soft brush or vacuum cleaner attachment to remove soot, then scrub with a hard scrubbing brush and clear warm water. If soiling does not respond, try wiping down with malt vinegar (this may also remove burn marks), followed by thorough rinsing. Heavy soot staining may need to be treated with a solution of spirits of salts (1 part spirits of salts to 6 parts water), but do not allow it to come into contact with the cement between the bricks. Wash down quickly and thoroughly with plenty of warm water. *Spirits of salts is corrosive*, so wear gloves and goggles and protect clothing; it also gives off extremely strong and *poisonous fumes*, so see that the room is well ventilated and do not lean over the surface while applying the solution.

On carpets Do not brush as this might spread the mark. Vacuum the area or shake the carpet or rug gently, out of doors if possible. Small marks will usually come out with an aerosol stain remover, such as **K2r**. Large areas of stain are best cleaned professionally, though they may respond to light brushing with the lather of a carpet shampoo solution. On light-coloured carpets, use repeated applications of French chalk or Fuller's Earth. Rub in lightly and vacuum off when the powder has absorbed the soot.

On stonework Follow fireplace manufacturer's cleaning instructions

when available. Otherwise scrub with clear water. Use a mild solution of washing-up liquid on light marks and a concentrated solution of domestic bleach on heavy marks. Rinse thoroughly.

Tar

On carpets and upholstery Scrape gently to remove the deposit. Very hard marks may be given an initial softening with a glycerine solution (equal parts glycerine and warm water). Leave for up to an hour then rinse with clear water and blot well. Use either a carpet spotting kit or, when dry, a stain remover, eg **Targon**, **Beaucaire**. Obstinate stains will sometimes respond to dabbing with eucalyptus oil, **Polyclens Plus** paint-brush cleaner or **Swarfega Hand Cleanser**, lightly rubbed into the pile.

Tea

On carpets Blot thoroughly. If the spill is recent, flush the area with a squirt from a soda syphon, or sponge with warm water. Blot well. When necessary, and where the tea contained milk, use a carpet shampoo. When dry, apply an aerosol stain remover, eg **K2r** if any traces remain. Dried tea stains should first be sponged with a laundry borax solution (15 ml borax to 500 ml warm water). If marking remains, rub in a glycerine solution (equal parts glycerine and warm water), leave for up to an hour, then rinse with clear water and use a carpet shampoo, following the manufacturer's instructions.

On upholstery Sponge with a laundry borax solution (15 ml borax to 500 ml warm water), then with clear water. Blot well. When dry, use an aerosol stain remover, eg **Goddard's Dry Clean** on any

Check first with safety rules on page 98

remaining traces. Alternatively, use an upholstery spotting kit.

Urine

On carpets Flush the area with a squirt from a soda syphon, or sponge with cold water and blot well. Sponge the damp area with carpet shampoo solution. Rinse several times with cold water with a few drops of antiseptic added. Blot well each time. Where a dried stain has affected the dye, sponge with an ammonia solution (15 ml ammonia to 500 ml cold water).

On mattresses This is more easily done by two people as the mattress is best turned on its side and held in position while treatment is carried out. Press a towel below the stained area and sponge with a cold solution of washing-up liquid or upholstery shampoo. Wipe with cold water to which you have added a few drops of antiseptic, eg **Dettol** or **Milton**. Alternatively, use an upholstery spotting kit. It is probable that a ring mark will remain, but full treatment is nonetheless necessary to remove the urine (which could cause the fabric to rot) and deodorise the area.

Vomit

On carpets With the bowl of a spoon, remove the deposit and flush the area with a squirt from a soda syphon. Blot well. Alternatively, sponge the area with a laundry borax solution (15 ml borax to 500 ml warm water). Blot well. Rub in the lather from a carpet shampoo solution. Repeat until stain has gone,

then rinse with warm water with a few drops of antiseptic added. Blot well. Alternatively, use a carpet spotting kit after removing the deposit.

On upholstery Spoon up the deposit. Sponge the affected area with warm water to which you have added a few drops of ammonia. Blot dry. Alternatively, use an upholstery spotting kit.

Wine

On carpets Flush the area with a squirt from a soda syphon, or sponge with warm water. Blot well. Rub over the area with carpet shampoo solution. Wipe with a cloth wrung out in clear water. Blot well. Repeat until clear. Alternatively, use a carpet spotting kit. A solution of glycerine and water (equal parts glycerine and warm water) can be left on the stain for up to 1 hour to clear any remaining trace. Rinse off and blot well. Sponging with methylated spirit may reduce old stains.

On upholstery Blot up as much as possible and sponge the area with warm clear water. Blot well. If a mark remains, sprinkle with French chalk or talcum powder while still damp. Brush off after a few minutes and continue to repeat applications until clear. Dried stains may need lubricating with a glycerine solution (equal parts glycerine and warm water), left for 15 minutes, then wiped with a cloth wrung out in warm detergent solution followed by clear water. Alternatively, use an upholstery spotting kit.

ADDRESSES FOR SPECIALISED STAIN REMOVING PRODUCTS

Brasso Solvent
Reckitt & Colman Ltd, Reckitt House, Stoneferry Road, Hull, North Humberside HU8 8DD.

Copydex Remover
Copydex Ltd, 1 Torquay Street, Harrow Road, London W2 5EL.

Holloway's Carpet Care Spot Removing Kit
G. E. Holloway & Son (Engineers) Ltd, 12 Carlisle Road, Colindale, London NW9 0HL, will supply the address of your nearest distributor (postal enquiries).

Holloway Chewing Gum Remover
As above.

Magica Rust Remover
Gerald Withers Marketing, London House, Friday Street, Minehead, Somerset.

RB70 Stain and Scale Remover
Celmac Distributors Ltd, Unit 3, Ferry Lane, Brentford, Middlesex TW8 0BG, will supply details of your nearest stockist; this product may also be ordered from them direct.

ServiceMaster First Aid Kit
Obtainable through local ServiceMaster Associates (see Yellow Pages). In case of difficulty, write to ServiceMaster Ltd, 50 Commercial Square, Freemans Common, Leicester LE2 7SR.

Choosing and using adhesives

Purpose	Adhesive	Application	Removal
1 Paper, thin card, photographs, cutting-out games for children	Use inexpensive thin glue or paste; many brands are sold at stationery shops. Examples: Gloy, UHU Gluepen.	Some brands squeeze out through a nozzle, others go on with a small brush. They dry quickly.	If still tacky, just wipe off. If the glue has dried, remove by soaking with warm water.
2 Most china, glass, pottery, earthenware, chunky jewellery, leather	Use a clear adhesive; these are usually made from synthetic rubber in a petroleum-based solvent. Water resistance varies so check before you buy. Examples: Bostik clear, UHU clear.	Apply with a spatula. All dry quickly.	Remove with acetone or nail-polish remover.
3 Metal, china or glass, where a particularly strong, water-resistant and heatproof bond is required	Use a two-part epoxy resin adhesive. These begin to set only when the two parts are mixed. Examples: Araldite, Bostik No. 7 Quick Set.	Mix equal volumes of resin and hardener and coat one or both surfaces lightly before putting them together. Setting times for the different adhesives vary; a quick version is available, sometimes referred to as '5-minute' or 'rapid', but the time can be up to six hours at room temperature. Bonding will be faster if you expose the mended article to a gentle heat. When mixing the adhesive, use a container and implement that you don't mind throwing away afterwards.	Wipe off extra adhesive with a cellulose thinner before it begins to set. When dry, epoxy resin adhesives are almost impossible to remove.
4 Bonding laminated plastic to wood, sticking hardboard panelling, etc. Any job where it is impossible to apply even pressure to hold the surfaces together while they bond	Use a contact adhesive. Basically similar to clear adhesives, these are sold in larger quantities for bigger jobs. They come in the form of thick liquids and give good water-resistance. On jobs where it may be difficult to be exact, use a type of contact adhesive that allows a small amount of initial movement for adjustment. Examples: Evo-Stik Impact, Bostik 3 Contact Adhesive.	Apply to both surfaces with a spatula or old knife and spread with a serrated comb to give even distribution. Some contact adhesives stick strongly the instant the two surfaces are brought together; as no adjustment is possible, use some kind of location guide to make sure you get the position exactly right.	Remove with white spirit or a solvent cleaner supplied by the manufacturer of the adhesive. *Use with care. The solvent is flammable and can be dangerous to inhale.*

Choosing and using adhesives (contd)

Purpose	Adhesive	Application	Removal
5 Upholstery, carpets and rugs	Use a latex adhesive, made from natural rubber in an emulsion with water. It comes as a thick, white liquid which dries to a translucent film giving strong, flexible joins. Example: Copydex.	Coat both surfaces and let them dry before pressing them together. Alternatively, coat one surface only and put them together at once.	Remove any surplus with a damp cloth while the latex is still wet. Once dry, latex is difficult to remove. You can try with white spirit, but the fabric may well be left with a residual stain. It is best to use the manufacturer's own solvent cleaner.
6 General indoor woodwork jobs and repairs	Use a PVA adhesive. These are based on polyvinyl acetate emulsions and are suitable for joining porous materials where a flexible join is unnecessary. Examples: Unibond Universal, Evo-Stik Woodworking Adhesive.	Spread the adhesive, which is white but dries clear, on to one surface only and assemble at once. Clamp the joint together until the adhesive is dry.	Wipe away all excess with a damp cloth while it is still tacky. PVA adhesives are difficult to remove when dry.
7 Outdoor woodwork and larger indoor jobs	For most outdoor woodwork, a urea-formaldehyde adhesive is recommended. These are usually synthetic resin powders that are mixed with water and undergo irreversible chemical changes on setting. The bond they form is heat-resistant, waterproof and very strong. Example: Cascamite.	Follow the directions carefully. Screw or clamp joints together until the adhesive is dry.	Cannot be removed.
8 Plastics	Most plastics except polythene and polypropylene can be successfully repaired with either a clear or contact adhesive. Some soft plastics such as PVC upholstery, airbeds, paddling pools, etc., can be difficult to mend. For these, vinyl adhesives have been specially formulated, usually designed to be used together with repair patches. Example: PVX.	For clear adhesives, see **2** opposite; for contact adhesives, see **4** opposite. When using a vinyl adhesive, follow the manufacturer's directions.	For clear adhesives, see **2** opposite; for contact adhesives, see **4** opposite. Follow the manufacturer's directions.

Choosing and using adhesives (contd) —

Purpose	Adhesive	Application	Removal
9 Fixing wall tiles	Use a wall tile adhesive, choosing a water resistant one for shower cubicles and similar installations. Example: Bal-Wall Ceramic Tile Adhesive.	Spread on the wall or on the tile, using a serrated comb to give even distribution. Work on a small area at a time as the adhesive dries quickly.	Remove any surplus of a standard adhesive with a wet cloth. For a water-resistant adhesive, use the manufacturer's own solvent.
10 Laying floor tiles	Use the adhesive recommended by the manufacturer of the floor covering.	Spread the adhesive on the floor with an old knife or spreader and 'work' with a large serrated comb.	Excess adhesive can be easily removed while it is still wet, but taking tiles up once the adhesive has hardened is a job for a professional. Take care not to let it dry on clothes or carpets as permanent damage is likely.

Super glues can be used to stick most of the items listed above, ie metal, rubber, glass, ceramics and most plastics. An example is Bostik 12, which is sold as a kit with a release agent in case you accidentally get it on your hands. Super glues are ideal for repairing small and awkwardly-shaped objects because they bond in about 30 seconds. As with most adhesives, super glues should be used in a well-ventilated area. Avoid contact with skin and eyes and avoid breathing in the vapours. Keep out of the reach of children.

Basic tool kit for minor repairs and maintenance

Hack saw
Tenon saw
Rip saw
Claw hammer
Cross-pein hammer
Large and small screwdrivers
    including Phillips or Pozidriv
Pliers
Plane or Surform rasp
Knife
Adjustable wrench
Adjustable spanner

Steel tape (3-metre length)
Ratchet brace and auger bits
Chisel
Glasspaper
Filler knife
Rags
Goggles
Gloves

Useful extra:
Power tool and attachments

Small tool kit

(to keep next to electrical mains switch and fuse box)

Insulated screwdriver
Torch
Pliers
Wire strippers

Knife
Card of fuse wire
Selection of 13-amp and 3-amp
    cartridge fuses*

* If your consumer unit takes cartridge fuses you should have 30-amp and 15-amp replacements for these.

Useful names and addresses

The following is a list of organisations to contact for advice and information.

**Association of British Launderers &
Cleaners**
Lancaster Gate House, 319 Pinner Road,
Harrow, Middlesex. *Tel: 01-863 7755*

Association of Master Upholsterers
Dormar House, Mitre Bridge, Scrubs Lane,
London NW10. *Tel: 01-205 0465*

Basketmakers' Association
Bierton House, Dean Way, Chalfont St.
Giles, Bucks.
Tel: Chalfont St. Giles (024 07) 2296

British Association of Removers
279 Gray's Inn Road, London WC1X 8SY.
Tel: 01-387 3088

**British Electrotechnical Approvals
Board (BEAB)**
Mark House, 9/11 Queens Road,
Hersham, Walton-on-Thames,
Surrey KT12 5NA.
Tel: Walton-on-Thames (09322) 44401

**British Furniture Manufacturers'
Federated Associations**
30 Harcourt Street, London W1H 2AA.
Tel: 01-724 0854

British Gas Corporation
Rivermill House, 152 Grosvenor Road,
London SW1V 3JL. *Tel: 01-821 1444*

British Insurance Association
Aldermary House, 10–15 Queen Street,
London EC4N 1TU. *Tel: 01-248 4477*
(send sae for leaflets on home security)

British Pest Control Association
Alembic House, 93 Albert Embankment,
London SE1 7TU. *Tel: 01-582 8268*

British Standards Institution
British Standards House, 2 Park Street,
London W1A 2BS. *Tel: 01-629 9000*

British Woodworking Federation
82 New Cavendish Street,
London W1M 8AD. *Tel: 01-580 5588*

The Building Centre
26 Store Street, London WC1E 7BT.
Tel: 01-637 8361

**Calor Gas Consumer Services
Department**
Calor House, Windsor Road, Slough,
Berks. SL1 2EQ. *Tel: Slough 23824*

Carpet Cleaners' Association
97 Knighton Fields Road West,
Leicester LE2 6LH.
Tel: Leicester (0533) 836065

**Consumers' Association (Publishers
of WHICH?)**
14 Buckingham Street,
London WC2N 6DS. *Tel: 01-839 1222*

**Council for Small Industries in Rural
Areas**
141 Castle Street, Salisbury, Wilts.
Tel: Salisbury (0722) 6255

Crown Decorative Advisory Bureau
Hollins Road, Darwen, Lancs. BB3 0BG.
Tel: Darwen (0254) 74951

Department of Energy
Information Division, Thames House
South, Millbank, London SW1P 4QJ.
Tel: 01-211 3000

The Design Centre
28 Haymarket, London SW1Y 4SU.
Tel: 01-839 8000

Electrical Association for Women
25 Foubert's Place, London W1V 2AL.
Tel: 01-437 5212

Electricity Council
30 Millbank, London SW1P 4RB.
Tel: 01-834 2333

Federation of Master Builders
33 John Street, London WC1.
Tel: 01-242 7583

Fire Protection Association
Aldermary House, 10–15 Queen Street,
London EC4N 1TU. *Tel: 01-248 5222*

Glass & Glazing Federation
6 Mount Row, London W1Y 6DY.
Tel: 01-409 0545

Guild of Master Craftsmen
10 Dover Street, London W1X 3PH.
Tel: 01-493 7571

Heating and Ventilating Contractors' Association
ESCA House, 34 Palace Court,
Bayswater, London W2 4JG.
Tel: 01-229 5543

ICI Hyde Products Ltd. (Novamura and Vymura Stockists and Advice)
PO Box 15, ICI, Newton Works, Hyde,
Cheshire. *Tel: 061-368 4000*
For information about their paints contact
the Retail Customer Service Office,
Decorative Paints Department, ICI Paints
Division, Wexham Road, Slough,
Berks. SL2 5DS. *Tel: Slough 31151*

Institute of Plumbing
Scottish Mutual House, North Street,
Hornchurch, Essex RM11 1RU.
Tel: Hornchurch 51236

Kitchen Specialists' Association
Turret House, Station Road, Amersham,
Bucks. *Tel: Amersham (024 03) 21431*

The National Bedding Federation
251 Brompton Road, London SW3 2EZ.
Tel: 01-589 4888

National Cavity Insulation Association
178–202 Great Portland Street,
London W1N 6AQ. *Tel: 01-637 7481*

National Consumer Council
18 Queen Anne's Gate,
London SW1H 9AA. *Tel: 01-222 9501*

National Federation of Roofing Contractors
15 Soho Square, London W1V 5FB.
Tel: 01-439 1753

National Fireplace Council
PO Box 35 (Stoke), Stoke-on-Trent,
Staffs. ST4 7HU.
Tel: Stoke-on-Trent (0782) 44311

National Gas Consumers' Council
130 Jermyn Street, London SW1Y 4UJ.
Tel: 01-930 7431

National Supervisory Council for Intruder Alarms
St. Ives House, St. Ives Road,
Maidenhead, Berks. SL6 1RD.
Tel: Maidenhead (0628) 37512

The Pianoforte Publicity Association
The Cloisters, 11 Salem Road,
London W2 4BU. *Tel: 01-221 0990*

Rentokil Advice Centre
(pest control and wood preservation)
Freepost, Felcourt, East Grinstead, West
Sussex. *Tel: East Grinstead (0342) 833022*

Royal Institute of British Architects
66 Portland Place, London W1N 4AD.
Tel: 01-323 0687

Royal Institution of Chartered Surveyors
12 Great George Street, Parliament
Square, London SW1P 3AD.
Tel: 01-222 7000

Royal Society for the Prevention of Accidents
Cannon House, The Priory Queensway,
Birmingham B4 6BS. *Tel: 021-233 2461*

Solar Trades Association
26 Store Street, London WC1E 7BT.
Tel: 01-636 4717

Solid Fuel Advisory Service
Hobart House, Grosvenor Place,
London SW1X 7AE. *Tel: 01-235 2020*

Timber Research & Development Association Ltd.
Stocking Lane, Hughenden Valley,
High Wycombe, Bucks. HP14 4ND.
Tel: Naphill (024 024) 3091

Specialist firms and services

If you are unable to carry out a repair yourself and need expert advice, the following specialist firms may be able to help.

BATHS
Renubath Services Ltd.
(in situ restoration)
The Old House, Calmsden, Cirencester, Glos. GL7 5ET.
Tel: Cirencester (0285) 66624

CANE AND RATTAN SUPPLIERS
The Eaton Bag Company Ltd.
(natural mattings, cane materials, cane roller blinds)
16 Manette Street, London W1V 5LB.
Tel: 01-437 9391

Jacob's, Young & Westbury Ltd.
JYW House, Bridge Road, Haywards Heath, West Sussex.
Tel: Haywards Heath (0444) 412411

CARPETS
Servicemaster Ltd.
(cleaning, retufting, soil proofing, static proofing, fire and flood restoration)
50 Commercial Square, Freemans Common, Leicester LE2 7SR.
Tel: Leicester (0533) 548620

Persian & Oriental Carpet Centre
(restoration and repair of oriental rugs)
63 South Audley Street,
London W1Y 5FB. *Tel: 01-629 9670*

Behar Profex Ltd.
(cleaning, conservation, valuing oriental rugs)
The Alban Building, St. Albans Place, Upper Street, London N1 0NX.
Tel: 01-226 0144

CHIMNEYS
The Chimney Specialists Ltd.
(general advice, faults and cures)
Jubilee Works, Chilton Industrial Estate, Sudbury, Suffolk.
Tel: Sudbury (0787) 75404

CHINA REPAIRS
Robin Hood Workshop
18 Bourne Street, Sloane Square, London SW1. *Tel: 01-730 0425*

Ashton-Bostock China Repairs
21 Charlwood Street, London SW1.
Tel: 01-828 3656

Thomas Goode & Co (London) Ltd.
19 South Audley Street,
London W1Y 6BN. *Tel: 01-499 2823*

CUTLERY REPAIRS (SILVER)
James W. Potter & Sons
10–12 Newbury Street, Whitchurch, Hants. *Tel: Whitchurch (025 682) 2983*

DAMP PROOFING
BP Aquaseal Ltd.
(products for damp proofing and helpful advice)
Kingsnorth Works, Hoo, Nr. Rochester, Kent ME3 9ND.
Tel: Medway (0634) 250722

Newtonite Ltd.
(damp-proof lining for walls)
160 Piccadilly, London W1V 0BX.
Tel: 01-237 1217

DOOR FURNITURE
J. D. Beardmore & Co. Ltd.
3 Percy Street, London W1.
Tel: 01-637 7041

Knobs & Knockers
61–65 Judd Street, London WC1.
Tel: 01-387 0091

Locks & Handles
Architectural Components Ltd.,
8 Exhibition Road, London SW7 2HF.
Tel: 01-584 6800

DOORS
From Door to Door
(period doors)
The Old Smithy, Cerrig-y-Drudion, Corwen, Clwyd.
Tel: Corwen (0490) 82491

Magnet & Southerns Ltd.
Royd Ings Avenue, Keighley, West Yorkshire. *Tel: Keighley (0535) 61133*

W. H. Newson & Sons Ltd.
61 Pimlico Road, London SW1.
Tel: 01-730 6262

GLASS
Bronson Shaw Design
(stained glass repair and design)
Granary Building, Hope Sufferance
Wharf, 61 St. Mary Church Street,
Rotherhithe, London SE16.
Tel: 01-994 3212

W. G. T. Burne Ltd.
*(blue glass liners and general repairs to
glass)*
11 Elystan Street, London SW3.
Tel: 01-589 6074

Thomas Goode & Co (London) Ltd.
19 South Audley Street,
London W1Y 6BN. *Tel: 01-499 2823*

R. Wilkinson & Son
45 Wastdale Road, Forest Hill,
London SE23. *Tel: 01-699 4420*

Beech & Son Ltd.
(clock domes)
Meridian House, Swanley, Kent.
Tel: Swanley 63211

LIGHTS
W. G. T. Burne Ltd.
(chandelier repairs)
11 Elystan Street, London SW3.
Tel: 01-589 6074

LOCKS
Banham's Patent Locks Ltd.
233 Kensington High Street,
London W8. *Tel: 01-937 4311*

MARBLE
Marble Works Ltd.
33 Gunnersbury Lane, London W3 8ED.
Tel: 01-992 1152/6111

A. Bell & Co. Ltd.
Thornton Road, Kingsthorpe,
Northampton.
Tel: Northampton (0604) 712505

METALS
J. D. Beardmore & Co.
(craftsmen in brass and copper)
Field End Road, Ruislip, Middlesex.
Tel: 01-864 6811

Foye Forge
*(copper, gold and silver plating of
flowers, bouquets, baby shoes, etc.)*
Station Road, Fowey, Cornwall.
Tel: Fowey (072 683) 2248

PLASTERWORK
Eaton Gaze Ltd.
(mouldings, columns, trusses, etc.)
86 Teesdale Street, Hackney Road,
London E2 6PU. *Tel: 01-739 7272*

**Moran & Wheatley (Ornamental
Plasterers) Ltd.**
Avonvale Studio, Avonvale Place,
Batheaston, Bath.
Tel: Bath (0225) 859678

ROOFS
Keymer Brick & Tile Co. Ltd.
*(hand-made clay roofing and cladding
tiles)*
Nye Road, Burgess Hill,
West Sussex RH15 0LZ.
Tel: Burgess Hill (044 46) 2931

Penrhyn Quarries Ltd.
*(natural slates in several colours, riven or
rubbed)*
Bethesday, Bangor, Gwynedd LL57 4YG.
Tel: Bangor (0248) 600656

Redland Re-Roofing Advice Centre
Freepost, Redland House, Reigate,
Surrey. *Tel: Reigate 42488*

Swallow's Tiles (Cranleigh) Ltd.
(hand-made roofing and cladding tiles)
Bookhurst Brick & Tile Works, Cranleigh,
Surrey GU6 7DP.
Tel: Cranleigh (048 66) 4100

Thatching Advisory Service
*(advice on thatch and thatching
problems; roof surveys, help in finding
thatchers, etc; Thatch Owners' Protection
Scheme on a membership basis)*
Rose Tree Farm, 29 Nine Mile Ride,
Wokingham, Berks.
Tel: Wokingham (0734) 734203

TILES (INTERIOR WALL TILES)
Ironbridge Gorge Museum
*(reproduction tiles from Victorian
originals)*
Maws Tile Works, Telford, Shropshire.
Tel: Telford (0952) 882030

H. & R. Johnson Tiles Ltd.
(reproduction Victorian tiles)
Stoke-on-Trent, Staffs.
Tel: Stoke-on-Trent (0782) 85611

TOY REPAIR
The Dolls' Hospital
*(dolls only—send an sae if writing for
information)*
16 Dawes Road, Fulham,
London SW6 7EN. *Tel: 01-385 2081*

Rallzo Rocking Horses
(rocking horse menders and restorers)
Old Yard Farm, North Bovey,
Newton Abbott, Devon.
Tel: Moretonhampstead (064 74) 423

Margaret Spencer
(rocking horse maker and mender)
Chard Road, Crewkerne,
Somerset TA18 8BA
Tel: Crewkerne (0460) 72362

UPHOLSTERY REPAIRS
House of Foam Ltd.
(upholstery requisites/everything for DIY)
62–64 Hoe Street, Walthamstow,
London E17. *Tel: 01-521 0596*

Royal School of Needlework
25 Princes Gate, London SW7 1QE.
Tel: 01-589 0077

Bridge of Weir Leather Co. Ltd.
*(leather desk top inserts, tooled if
required)*
Clydesdale Works, Bridge of Weir,
Renfrewshire PA11 3LF.
Tel: Bridge of Weir (0505) 612132

WINDOWS
Allan Bros.
*(reproduction Georgian timber sashes,
glazing bars to order)*
PO Box 5, Tweed Saw Mills,
Berwick-upon-Tweed TD15 2A7.
Tel: Berwick-upon-Tweed (0289) 7443

Boulton & Paul Joinery Ltd.
*(glazing bars, double-hung sash
windows)*
Riverside Works, Norwich NR1 1EB.
Tel: Norwich (0603) 60133

W. H. Newson Ltd.
(Georgian-style sash windows)
61 Pimlico Road, London SW1.
Tel: 01-730 6262

INDEX